Editors
Erica N. Russikoff, M.A.
Mary S. Jones, M.A.

Editor in Chief
Karen J. Goldfluss, M.S. Ed.

Cover Artist
Tony Carrillo

Art Coordinator
Renée Mc Elwee

Illustrator
Clint McKnight

Imaging
James Edward Grace
Leonard P. Swierski

Publisher
Mary D. Smith, M.S. Ed.

DAILY WARM-UPS

TCR 3978

Nonfiction & Fiction

Writing

5

Includes:

➤ *150 writing activities that target six writing traits*

➤ *engaging nonfiction and fiction writing topics*

➤ *writing prompts for additional practice*

➤ *standards and benchmarks*

Ideas and Content
Word Choice
Fluency
Voice
Organization
Conventions

Focused, fun writing practice every day!

Teacher Created Resources

Author

Ruth Foster, M. Ed.

The classroom teacher may reproduce copies of the materials in this book for use in a single classroom only. The reproduction of any part of the book for other classrooms or for an entire school or school system is strictly prohibited. No part of this publication may be transmitted, stored, or recorded in any form without written permission from the publisher.

Teacher Created Resources
6421 Industry Way
Westminster, CA 92683
www.teachercreated.com

ISBN: 978-1-4206-3978-0

© *2012 Teacher Created Resources*
Made in U.S.A.

Teacher Created Resources

Table of Contents

Introduction

The written word is a valuable and mighty tool. It allows us to communicate ideas, thoughts, feelings, and information. As with any tool, skill comes with practice. *Daily Warm-Ups: Nonfiction and Fiction Writing* uses high-interest and grade-level appropriate exercises to help develop confident, skillful writers.

This book is divided into seven sections. Each of the first six sections focuses on one of the following key writing traits. These traits have been identified by teachers as effective tools for improving student writing. The last section in the book offers a set of writing prompts to encourage further writing opportunities throughout the year.

Nonfiction and Fiction—Writing Traits Focus

★ IDEAS and CONTENT

★ VOICE

★ WORD CHOICE

★ ORGANIZATION

★ FLUENCY

★ CONVENTIONS

Daily Warm-Ups: Nonfiction and Fiction Writing uses a format that allows for flexibility in both instruction and learning. You may wish to begin with Warm-Up 1 and progress sequentially through all or most of the writing practices provided in the book. As an alternative, begin by introducing and modeling a specific writing trait that needs to be addressed. Students can then use the warm-ups within that section to practice and apply the trait as they complete each of the writing activities. Once the section is completed, continue working through the remaining sections based on the needs of the class.

With 150 independent warm-ups, there are plenty of writing opportunities to last the entire school year. As with any subject to be learned and mastered, writing should be continually practiced. With an arsenal of good writing techniques and an understanding of the writing process at their disposal, students can achieve a comfort level regardless of the writing task. Daily writing and guided practice using essential writing traits can help students reach a measurable level of success.

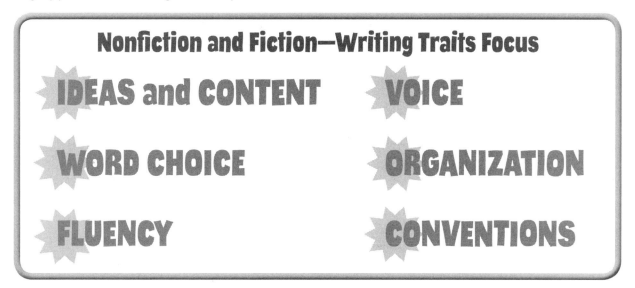

About This Book

The activities in this book were designed to help students gain experience writing in response to both nonfiction and fiction prompts. Each topic or theme includes pages that address both fiction and nonfiction writing.

The warm-up activities allow students to use both nonfiction and fiction writing on the same topic!

These pages are about curfews. The first warm-up presents nonfiction information and asks the writer to prepare a response using the facts and ideas provided.

The second warm-up introduces the same topic in the form of a scenario and requires the student to write a story.

The writing exercises in this book give students the opportunity to use a variety of writing formats. This allows a student to practice a specific writing skill while developing an understanding that good writing traits can be incorporated into a number of genres. The variation also keeps the daily writing activities exciting.

Each of the first six sections contains 25 warm-up writing pages that focus on the specific trait featured in the section.

The activities are written so that all students in a class can participate. While highly competent students may write more complex responses, all students will be able to practice writing at their respective levels of competence on a daily basis.

Each section ends with a page that incorporates both nonfiction and fiction writing activities. This page can be used as a culminating activity for the section, or as an informal assessment representative of the student's writing using the specific writing trait.

Space has been provided for students to write their responses on the activity page. For instances in which students need additional space to complete an activity, use the back of the page, or continue on separate paper. Encourage students to use a notebook where they can extend their writing or create new writing pieces if they choose to do so.

The last section of the book includes a set of writing prompts that can be used throughout the year. These provide ideas, story starters, and a variety of scenarios for students to use as prompts. Students (or the teacher) can select one prompt a week to use as a topic for their writing. As an alternative, select a prompt and ask students to focus on one or two specific traits as they write. There are many ways to use these prompts. Choose a method that works best for you and your students.

Good Writing Traits

Ideas and Content . . . .

This trait lays the foundation for other aspects of effective student writing. Students need to learn to develop and organize their ideas and present them clearly. Students should gather their ideas, as well as research, seek new knowledge, and organize their information, before they begin to write. Successful writers write about what they know, the subjects in which they have expertise, or specific knowledge and experience.

In practicing the characteristics of this trait, students identify topics about which they have prior knowledge, investigate and explore topics further by conducting additional research if needed, and learn to connect their writing to their own experiences.

Writing that is strong in content includes interesting, relevant, specific details and a development of the piece as a whole. Students should have opportunities to practice organizing their ideas, writing about their own experiences, using examples and details, and writing complete pieces. This allows them to use insight and understanding to show readers what they know.

Word Choice . . . .

Paying attention to word choice enables students to write effectively so the reader will understand and want to read their writing. Elements of the word-choice trait include using strong visual imagery and descriptive writing.

Writers learn to use accurate and precise words to say exactly what they want to communicate. Specific words convey distinct meanings. Students should use action words, as well as descriptive nouns and adjectives, to give their writing energy.

Using effective word choice implies a familiarity with the language as students learn to use parts of speech and subject-verb agreement properly. An effective writer listens to how words sound, using words that sound natural and add to the meaning of the writing.

As students become more adept at choosing the right words to express their intent, their written communication will be more easily understood and enjoyable to read.

Fluency . . . .

As students learn to incorporate the trait of fluency into their writing, they should continue to practice what they learned about the word-choice trait. As writers develop fluency, they play with different word patterns and use words to match the mood of their writing. Fluent writing contains sentences varying in length and structure.

Students should learn to express themselves in clear sentences that make sense. This will happen as they incorporate natural rhythm and flow into their writing, making sure that ideas begin purposefully and connect to one another.

A writer may engage in a process of thinking that begins by asking the question, "What if?" One question leads to another, and the writer begins to develop smooth transitions and pacing. Mastery of each component of the fluency trait leads to a final outcome—the ability to pass a read aloud test.

As students learn about the fluency trait, they should practice ways to express themselves by writing in a variety of formats. They will gather words to create word patterns and match specific moods.

Good Writing Traits *(cont.)*

Voice

As students gain confidence using the trait of fluency, they begin to learn about writing style. The voice trait focuses specifically on a writer's individual style. An effective piece of writing that exhibits aspects of the voice trait will sound like a particular person wrote it. Therefore, writing that has characteristics of voice will also be fluent; it will have natural rhythm. Authors develop their own unique style by writing from their thoughts and feelings. An author's personality comes through in his or her writing. Effective writers focus on their audience—they write to the reader. They want to call attention to the writing and draw the reader in. To do this, authors will write honestly, sincerely, and with confidence. As they write based on their own experiences and knowledge of themselves, writers will have the ability to bring a topic to life.

Students should continue to practice expanding their perspectives, as well as read sample pieces written from another person's point of view. By doing so, they will learn to identify elements of the voice trait in written samples and begin to develop their own style by writing reflections and personal correspondence.

Organization

Once students learn to incorporate the organization trait in their writing, they begin to view the whole picture. Effective writing has a logical order and sequence with clear direction and purpose; it does not confuse the reader. Rather, writing that displays qualities of organization guides the reader through the writing, leading to the main point. Writers who incorporate the characteristics of the organization trait include an introduction that captures the reader's attention and conclude the piece by making the reader think. Organized writing flows smoothly, with transitions that tie together.

Students can practice the characteristics of this trait by learning about beginnings and endings of stories and paragraph structure. They should practice writing their own paragraphs. The teacher can assist by introducing story elements to the students and giving them opportunities to outline a story, identify story elements, and write a complete story. As students learn to organize their written work, they begin to focus on appropriate pacing and transitions in their writing, leading to a more cohesive and readable final product.

Conventions

Students put the pieces together as they worked through the organization trait and began to consider the whole picture. They also had opportunities to consider self-evaluation, based on established criteria. The next major step in the writing process is editing. The conventions trait breaks the huge task of editing into smaller parts—allowing students to practice editing their own and others' work, focusing on one factor at a time.

Students learn about and practice correct forms of conventions such as correctly spelling plural and singular forms of nouns, capitalization of place names, punctuation, possessives, and subject-verb agreement. While students often practice characteristics of the conventions trait by reading and editing samples written by others, it is important that they continually edit their own work.

Good Writing Traits *(cont.)*

Presentation

The trait of presentation refers to the publication part of the writing process. After students have completed a written piece, they present it to their audience: visually, orally, or using both formats. The presentation trait consists of two components: visual and auditory.

Students consider appropriate visual formats for their writing, as well as the use of color. Visual aids include charts, diagrams, and graphs. The visuals may include text. Specifically, students learn how to create a graph for a presentation.

The auditory component of presentation includes presenting work in an oral format; students learn public-speaking skills through drama and critique. Practicing this trait also gives students the opportunity to speak about personal experiences, ask and respond to questions, and clearly state their main points when presenting their writing to others.

 **A NOTE ABOUT PRESENTATION**

While presentation is not included among the sections of this book, it should still be considered an important trait. The goal of the activities in this book is to provide relatively short, daily warm-up practice. The presentation process involves additional time and preparation. However, you can periodically allow students to display and present some of their writing to an audience with a focus on good visual and auditory techniques.

EVALUATING THE EFFECTIVE USE OF TRAITS IN THE WRITING WARM-UPS

A sample scoring rubric is provided on page 8. Each trait can be presented individually so that it can be used to help students as they first learn about the Good Writing Traits, or page 8 can be passed out in its entirety to serve as a reference.

Use each rubric trait by itself to score writing from that section or combine traits to match special assignments. You can also teach the traits in a cumulative manner, adding one trait to your rubric as you begin each section. Another option is to create your own descriptions using page 8 as an example. Yet another alternative is to include students in the process by creating a rubric with them based on their growing understanding of each trait.

Before using any rubric, make sure students are aware of the criteria for which they will be assessed. Model sample writing pieces using the trait and criteria prior to using the rubric as a tool for evaluation. Keep in mind that a rubric is flexible and can be adapted for specific writing practice or group warm-ups. It is an effective and relatively quick way to assess student progress.

Sample Scoring Rubric

	4	**3**	**2**	**1**
Ideas and Content	The writing's central idea is clear and focused, and it is supported by vivid, relevant details.	The writer has defined a topic, but it is supported by few details.	There is a topic, but it is not clearly defined. Some details may be related.	The writer has not defined a topic; details are lacking or irrelevant.
Word Choice	The writer uses precise, natural, and engaging words to convey the intended message.	The writer has made the meaning clear, and some word choices are engaging and match the purpose.	While the writer's meaning is clear, word choice is basic or not appropriate for the message and audience.	Words are used incorrectly, or the writer uses such limited vocabulary that meaning is impaired.
Fluency	Sentence length and structure are varied, and the writing flows well.	The writing can be read aloud easily. In some places, the writing flows well.	The writing is mechanical rather than musical.	The writing can be read aloud only with practice. Many structural problems exist.
Voice	The writing is tailored for the intended audience, with an engaging and lively tone.	The writing is somewhat tailored for the intended audience. The tone may be inconsistent.	While functional, the voice is impersonal; the piece could have been written by anybody.	The writer seems indifferent to his or her audience or topic; readers are not moved.
Organization	Organization supports the topic and clearly moves the reader through the text.	The organizational structure is clear, though there are better alternatives.	Readers find meaning without confusion, but their path is indirect.	There is no clear structure. Events and information seem random.
Conventions	Complex conventions enhance meaning and readability. Errors are few.	The writer has control of the basic conventions but struggles to use anything more complex.	Errors are distracting. Only simple conventions are used.	Errors make the piece difficult to read. The writer incorrectly uses basic conventions.
Presentation	Layout and presentation enhance meaning and visual appeal.	The writing is readable and neat, neither adding to nor detracting from meaning and appeal.	Presentation is somewhat messy, detracting from appeal but not meaning.	Presentation is distracting or messy, making the meaning unclear.

Standards for Writing

Each activity in *Daily Warm-Ups: Nonfiction & Fiction Writing* meets at least one of the following standards and benchmarks, which are used with permission from McREL. Copyright 2012 McREL. Mid-continent Research for Education and Learning, 4601 DTC Boulevard, Suite 500, Denver, Colorado 80237. Telephone: 303-337-0990. Website: *www.mcrel.org/standards-benchmarks*. To align McREL Standards to the Common Core Standards, go to *www.mcrel.org*.

Uses the general skills and strategies of the writing process

1. Prewriting: Uses prewriting strategies to plan written work (e.g., uses graphic organizers, story maps, and webs; groups related ideas; takes notes; brainstorms ideas; organizes information according to type and purpose of writing)

3. Editing and Publishing: Uses strategies to edit and publish written work (e.g., edits for grammar, punctuation, capitalization, and spelling at a developmentally appropriate level; uses reference materials; excludes extraneous details and inconsistencies; selects presentation format according to purpose; uses available technology to publish work)

5. Uses strategies (e.g., adapts focus, organization, point of view; determines knowledge and interests of audience) to write for different audiences (e.g., self, peers, teachers, adults)

6. Uses strategies (e.g., adapts focus, point of view, organization, form) to write for a variety of purposes (e.g., to inform, entertain, explain, describe, record ideas)

7. Writes expository compositions (e.g., identifies and stays on the topic; develops the topic with simple facts, concrete details, examples, definitions, quotations, and explanations; uses domain-specific or content area vocabulary; excludes extraneous and inappropriate information; uses logical organizing structures such as cause-and-effect, chronology, similarities and differences; uses several sources of information; provides a concluding statement)

8. Writes narrative accounts, such as poems and stories (e.g., establishes a context that enables the reader to imagine the event or experience; develops characters, setting, and plot; creates an organizing structure; uses transitions to sequence events; uses concrete sensory details; uses strategies such as dialogue, tension, and suspense; uses an identifiable voice)

9. Writes autobiographical compositions (e.g., provides a context within which the incident occurs, uses simple narrative strategies, and provides some insight into why this incident is memorable)

10. Writes expressive compositions (e.g., expresses ideas, reflections, and observations; uses an individual, authentic voice; uses narrative strategies, relevant details, and ideas that enable the reader to imagine the world of the event or experience)

11. Writes in response to literature (e.g., summarizes main ideas and significant details; relates own ideas to supporting details; advances judgments; supports judgments with references to the text, other works, other authors, nonprint media, and personal knowledge)

12. Writes personal letters (e.g., includes the date, address, greeting, body, and closing)

Uses the stylistic and rhetorical aspects of writing

1. Uses descriptive and precise language that clarifies and enhances ideas (e.g., concrete words and phrases, common figures of speech, sensory details)

2. Uses paragraph form in writing (e.g., indents the first word of a paragraph, uses topic sentences, recognizes a paragraph as a group of sentences about one main idea, uses an introductory and concluding paragraph, writes several related paragraphs)

3. Uses a variety of sentence structures in writing (e.g., expands basic sentence patterns, uses exclamatory and imperative sentences)

Uses grammatical and mechanical conventions in written compositions

2. Uses pronouns in written compositions (e.g., substitutes pronouns for nouns, uses pronoun agreement)

3. Uses nouns in written compositions (e.g., uses plural and singular naming words, forms regular and irregular plurals of nouns, uses common and proper nouns, uses nouns as subjects, uses abstract nouns)

4. Uses verbs in written compositions (e.g., uses a wide variety of action verbs, past and present verb tenses, simple tenses, forms of regular verbs, verbs that agree with the subject)

5. Uses adjectives in written compositions (e.g., indefinite, numerical and predicate adjectives; uses conventional patterns to order adjectives)

6. Uses adverbs in written compositions (e.g., to make comparisons)

7. Links ideas using connecting words (e.g., uses coordinating conjunctions in written compositions)

9. Uses conventions of spelling in written compositions (e.g., spells high-frequency, commonly misspelled words from appropriate grade-level list; uses a dictionary and other resources to spell words; uses initial consonant substitution to spell related words; uses vowel combinations for correct spelling; uses contractions, compounds, roots, suffixes, prefixes, and syllable constructions to spell words)

10. Uses conventions of capitalization in written compositions (e.g., titles of people; proper nouns [names of towns, cities, counties, and states; days of the week; months of the year; names of streets; names of countries; holidays]; first word of direct quotations; heading, salutation, and closing of a letter)

11. Uses conventions of punctuation in written compositions (e.g., uses periods after imperative sentences and in initials, abbreviations, and titles before names; uses commas in dates and addresses and after greetings and closings in a letter; uses apostrophes in contractions and possessive nouns; uses quotation marks around titles and with a comma for direct quotations; uses a colon between hour and minutes; use commas for tag questions, direct address, and to set off words)

Ideas and Content

What do you know about koalas? Is a baby koala bigger or smaller than a nickel? How is a koala like a kangaroo? You can research koalas in books or on the Internet using a search engine.

Koalas and kangaroos are both marsupials. Marsupials are mammals that have pouches on the females for carrying the young. Marsupial babies crawl into their mothers' pouches after birth. Inside the pouches, they drink milk and grow.

When a koala is born, it is smaller than a nickel! The koala is not fully formed, as it is blind and deaf. It takes a baby koala about five minutes to crawl inside its mother's pouch. Once inside, it will not come out for six months. When a baby koala is born, its back legs are just beginning to take shape. In contrast, its front legs are quite strong.

Activity: Write a paragraph in which you include some koala facts. Then tell one reason why the koala might need to have strong front legs. Think: What does it have to do after it is born?

_____

_____

_____

_____

_____

_____

_____

_____

_____

_____

_____

The Two-Headed Animal

DID YOU KNOW? A baby koala can return to its mother's pouch for two months after it first comes out. Then it gets too big to fit. Most marsupials have pouches that open toward the front (mother's head). The koala is different. The pouch opens up towards the back (mother's bottom)!

Activity: Write a story in which someone is sure they have seen a two-headed animal. Although, what they are really seeing is a mother koala with its baby sticking its head out of her pouch! Will your story be present day or long ago? It is your choice. Don't forget to include a title!

_____

_____

_____

_____

_____

_____

_____

_____

_____

_____

_____

_____

_____

_____

The Koala and You

Activity: Compare and contrast yourself to a koala. Use information you already know about the koala and the koala facts below.

Koala Facts

- two thumbs on each hand
- nocturnal (active at night)
- eats about 2.5 pounds of eucalyptus leaves per day
- weighs between 10 and 30 pounds
- gets most of its water from leaves so can go months without drinking any water
- average 2 feet long
- not comfortable on the ground
- tree-living, but can swim!

Me   Both   Koala

Swim
Climb
thumbs

The Missing Koala

IMAGINE THAT!

A koala has gone missing from the zoo. You talk to a suspect and he says, "This isn't the missing koala from the zoo. This is my pet koala. I have had it for two years. Now, if you will excuse me, I need to feed my koala."

Activity: Write two paragraphs about the situation above. In the first paragraph, have the suspect describe the different foods he feeds the koala. Include many details! Have the suspect talk about where he buys the food, how he prepares it, and how much the koala eats. Also, have him describe the koala's favorite food. Use what you know about what people feed their pets in this paragraph to make it sound believable.

In the second paragraph, have the detective tell the suspect why he knows the koala does not belong to the suspect. Koalas only eat eucalyptus leaves! They eat about 2.5 pounds of leaves a day! The suspect never said he was going to feed the koala eucalyptus leaves.

_____

_____

_____

_____

_____

_____

_____

_____

_____

_____

_____

_____

_____

Bad Mood

THINK ABOUT IT! People think koalas are cuddly and friendly, but this is not always the case. Sometimes koalas are in a bad mood. How can one tell? When koalas are in a bad mood, they will sometimes make a very loud and fast ticking sound.

Activity: Think of a time in your own life when you were in a bad mood. Include many details. Tell what put you in the bad mood. Describe what you did, said, or looked like when you were in this bad mood. Explain how you got out of your bad mood. Is there anything you can do to try and stop bad moods before they happen?

_____

_____

_____

_____

_____

_____

_____

_____

_____

_____

_____

_____

_____

_____

Tasmanian Tiger

DID YOU KNOW?

The Tasmanian tiger is also known as the Tasmanian wolf. The animal looks like a dog or wolf with stripes. However, this animal is not a wolf, dog, or tiger. Rather, it is a meat-eating marsupial! The Tasmanian tiger is extinct. The last one was spotted in Tasmania, Australia, in the 1930s. Some say that this animal might still be alive. Rewards have been offered for this animal's safe capture as valid proof. Some rewards have been more than one million dollars!

Activity: Write a story about a child who is in a bad mood. You decide what puts the child in a bad mood. Have the child go off to be by himself or herself. The child then makes friends with a dog that turns out to be a Tasmanian tiger!

It is your story, so you choose when and how the child finds out what the new friend really is. Tell what the child does when he or she finds out. Does the animal stay in the wild, or is it taken to a zoo?

_____

_____

_____

_____

_____

_____

_____

_____

_____

_____

_____

Kangaroo Talk

Ideas and Content

THINK ABOUT IT! News reporters interview people. The reporters will think of and decide on questions to ask ahead of time. This helps them find out what they want to know, and it also helps them keep the conversation flowing.

Activity: Write a news interview between you and a biologist who studies kangaroos. Use the information in the box below to help you write some questions and answers.

First, greet your audience, and then introduce yourself and your guest. Include words and phrases that make the conversation flow. Include what you know about kangaroos, too. Adding your own thoughts, feelings, or jokes will help your audience feel as if they are in the room during the interview.

Remember to put a colon (:) after the name of the person who is talking. (You can make up any name you want for the biologist.) Continue your news interview on another sheet of paper.

Kangaroo Facts

- Big ones can jump farther than any other animal.
- Some can jump 44 feet in a single bound and over an 11-foot fence.
- Big kangaroos can go 40 miles per hour.
- It is the only known animal that uses less energy the faster it goes because of the way it recycles energy through its legs' tendons!
- The babies are called *joeys*.
- Desert kangaroos can live on less water than camels.
- They are excellent swimmers.

_____ : _____
(Your name)

_____ : _____
(Biologist)

_____

_____

_____

_____

Platypus on the Radio

IMAGINE THAT!

Imagine that you are interviewing a duck-billed platypus for a radio show.

Activity: Think of questions to ask the platypus. Include your thoughts and interesting comments so that people will want to stay and listen. You can make your platypus silly, sad, or serious.

Use information in the box to help you come up with some questions. Make sure to introduce yourself and your guest! Share your radio station information, too. Remember to separate the person or thing speaking from what he or she says with a colon (:).

Platypus Facts

- It is a mammal with hair and milk.
- It lays eggs.
- It has a bill and webbed feet like a duck.
- It has a tail like a beaver.
- It lives in Australia.
- It can stay underwater for 10 minutes.
- It only weighs about four pounds but may eat two pounds of food a day!

_____

_____

_____

_____

_____

_____

_____

_____

_____

_____

Mystery Person

Activity: Think of a real person and write two paragraphs about him or her. Describe the person in detail in the first paragraph. Tell what they look like (size, hair) and how they are often dressed. In the second paragraph, tell what the person likes or does. Give examples that support what you say.

The person may be close to you or someone famous. End your paragraph with the line, "Who is this person? This person is _____." Write the answer on the back of the page.

Example sentences filled with details:

Her teeth are like white pearls, and you see them often because she is always smiling.

He gets so wrapped up when he is playing games that he doesn't notice what is going on around him. One time . . .

He really likes to kid around and play jokes on people. One time . . .

Mystery Game

DID YOU KNOW? Many writers make up characters and games. For example, J.K. Rowling wrote books about a boy wizard named Harry Potter. Harry played a game called *quidditch*. In quidditch, there are two teams of seven players. In the game, the players ride on flying broomsticks and use four balls.

Activity: Make up a game, give it a name, and then describe how to play it. Do teams or individuals compete? Is there a ball or a bat? What are the rules, and how does one get points? What is a foul? Give examples. What is a winning score? Your game can be silly, difficult, or fun. It can be played in any location and using any kind of sports equipment.

The Great State

THINK ABOUT IT!

There are 50 states in the United States of America. What makes your state different from the other states?

Activity: Write a letter to a friend, telling him or her what makes your state special. Tell what you like best about your state. Include state facts in your letter, including what animals might be seen in your state.

Dear _____,

_____

_____

_____

_____

_____

_____

_____

_____

_____

_____

_____

Your friend,

_____

Pen Pal from South Australia

IMAGINE THAT! Imagine that you have a pen pal in Australia. Your pen pal lives by Lake Torrens in South Australia. Lake Torrens is 2,200 square miles.

Activity: Write two postcards. The first postcard should be from you to your friend. Tell your friend how lucky he or she is to live by such a huge lake. Tell your friend the kinds of things you like to do or would like to do in a big lake.

The second postcard should be written by your pen pal **after** he or she gets your card. It is his or her response to you. When you write as an Australian, think about the following:

- Close friends are called *mates*.
- Lake Torrens is a dry, salt flat. In the last 150 years, it has only been filled with water once!

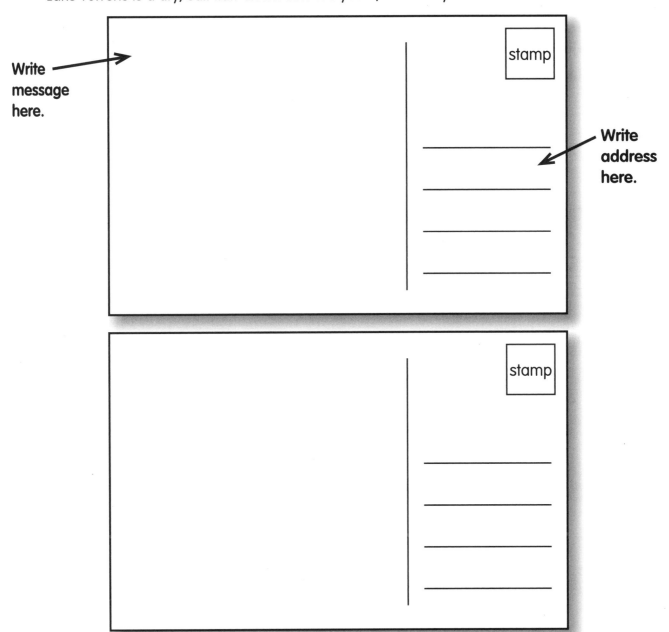

Write message here.

stamp

Write address here.

stamp

THINK ABOUT IT!

There is a new student in class who is not sure how to multiply. The student comes to you and says, "The problem says to find the product of 24 times 9. What is a product? Do you add when it says 'times' or do you subtract? Can you help me?"

Activity: Help the new student find the product of 24 times 9 by listing "how-to" steps. Write a title for your steps. One step should tell what a product is. Another step should show how to rewrite 24 x 9 in vertical form.

The Crawl

IMAGINE THAT!

There are several different kinds of swimming strokes. The fastest is known as the crawl, front crawl, or freestyle. Imagine that a friend comes to visit you. The friend lives in the dry desert and barely knows how to swim. He listens to you describe the crawl, and then he jumps into the shallow end of your pool. He then gets on his back and waves his hands in the air!

Next, he puts his head under the water and tries to breathe through his nose! You realize you must give him another lesson. This time, you make a chart. You break the swimming lesson into steps.

Activity: Write a lesson for the crawl stroke. Break it down into steps so that even someone who is new to swimming will know what to do!

The Bucket Sale

THINK ABOUT IT! Advertisers want you to buy their products. Some advertisers use examples that show the buyer new ways to use their products. For example, a shoe company may show an athlete playing a sports game while wearing their shoes.

Activity: What if you were writing an ad for a plastic bucket? You would need to come up with some fun and interesting examples of how it could be used. Write down two examples of how the plastic bucket can be used. Your examples can be serious, silly, or wild. Each example should include at least five lines and be filled with details. Use your imagination and have fun!

Example: *A woman is floating on a life raft in the middle of the ocean. All of a sudden, a shark, with its mouth open, comes charging toward her on the raft! It looks as if she is doomed! Then the woman picks up a large plastic bucket. She quickly thrusts the bucket in front of the shark, and the shark rams its head into it. The bucket gets stuck on the shark's head, and the shark can't bite anything! The trusty plastic bucket has saved the day!*

_____

_____

_____

_____

_____

_____

_____

_____

_____

Corn Flakes

DID YOU KNOW?

In 1894, Corn Flakes® were invented by accident. Dr. John Kellogg and his brother were making food for their patients. They accidentally let some cooked wheat go stale. They tried to use it anyway, and it came out as small flakes. They toasted the flakes, and cereal was invented! Later, corn was used instead of wheat.

Activity: Now it is your turn to create a new food. Tell what it is, how it tastes, and how it is made. Give details about how it was invented. Make up a name for the new food, too. Tell why people might want to or should buy your food. Your food can be wild, serious, healthy, sweet, or magical. Use your imagination!

_____

_____

_____

_____

_____

_____

_____

_____

_____

_____

_____

_____

_____

Marco Polo, Coal, and Bamboo

DID YOU KNOW?

Many explorers kept diaries. Then they wrote books about what they saw, did, and felt. Marco Polo lived from 1254 to 1324. He left Venice, Italy, in 1271 and headed for Asia.

Activity: Write two diary entries for Polo. Discuss when Polo first saw the following:

Entry 1

- people bathing every day
- using "black stones which they dig out and burn like firewood" (When Polo was alive, Europeans did not bathe very often. The black stones were coal.)

Entry 2

- people throwing bamboo onto fires to scare wild animals (Bamboo is hollow inside. When heated, the air inside expands. This makes the bamboo explode with a loud pop or crack.)

Date _____: _____

_____

_____

_____

_____

Date _____: _____

_____

_____

_____

_____

22

The Fastest-Growing Plant

IMAGINE THAT! Bamboo is one of the fastest-growing plants in the world. Some types of bamboo can grow 39 inches in a day! Some bamboo plants grow to be nearly 100 feet tall.

Activity: Imagine a person who sees some seedlings, digs them up, and replants them in his or her yard. Write three diary entries for this person. Include his or her thoughts and feelings. The person does not know it, but he or she has planted the fastest-growing bamboo! You choose the time between each written entry.

DID YOU KNOW?

A curfew is how late you can legally stay out in a public place. The word *curfew* came from the French word *couvre-feu*. In English, it means *cover-fire*. Long ago, around 1066, William the Conqueror started the first curfew law. A bell was rung in the evening that meant it was time for everyone to put out or cover their home fires. This helped keep people safe and homes and cities from burning.

Today some cities have curfew laws. Some curfew laws are for everyone; others are only for certain nights or only for children and teenagers. These laws are intended to keep people safe.

Activity: Write two paragraphs about curfews. In the first paragraph, explain what a curfew is and how it came about. Give an example of a time when an emergency curfew might be needed.

In the second paragraph, tell if your city has one and what it is. Then state if you agree or disagree. If there was a curfew, what times and days should they be? Who should it be for? What should the penalty be if someone breaks a curfew? How about if he or she breaks it more than once?

24

The Visitor and the Curfew

Activity: Write a story about a new visitor to a town. The town is small and has a temporary curfew. The curfew is in place because some animal has escaped from the zoo or circus (or a wild animal has wandered into town). The visitor who comes to the town thinks that he or she is superior to everyone in the town. People try to tell the visitor about the curfew, but the visitor just laughs. The visitor thinks the townspeople are just afraid to have fun. What will happen to the visitor in your story?

Fill your story with details: where is the town, and why is there a curfew? Where is the visitor from, and what are some of his or her characteristics? Who tries to warn the visitor? What happens to the visitor? Don't forget to include a title!

_____

_____

_____

_____

_____

_____

_____

_____

_____

_____

_____

Bio Poems

DID YOU KNOW?

A Bio Poem is like a biography. It is about a person, animal, or fictional character.

Activity: Write a nonfiction Bio Poem about yourself. Then write a fictional one about a character from a book, story, cartoon, or show. See the poem outline and example below.

Line 1: First name	Pete
Line 2: Four descriptive traits	Feathery, bright, beautiful, vain
Line 3: Sibling or child of . . .	Brother of Terry Turkey and Edgar Emu,
Line 4: Who loves or likes. . .	Lover of beauty shows and posing,
Line 5: Who fears . . .	Fears tail-snatchers and coyotes,
Line 6: Who needs . . .	Needs to strut and look proud,
Line 7: Who gives . . .	Gives color to the world,
Line 8: Who would like to see . . .	Would like to see an ostrich fly,
Line 9: Resident of . . .	Resident of Bird Park, Eagleton
Line 10: Last name	Peacock.

Yourself

_____

_____

_____

_____

_____

_____

_____

_____

_____

Character

_____

_____

_____

_____

_____

_____

_____

_____

_____

Word Choice

Bad or Atrocious?

THINK ABOUT IT!

If something is bad or atrocious, it is not good or nice. Does it matter which word a writer uses: *bad* or *atrocious*? Yes, it does matter. This is because the writer can set a mood by helping the reader feel a certain way. The writer can help the reader form a better picture in his or her mind. When something is *atrocious*, it is really bad, awful, horrid, and dreadful.

Activity: Compare each phrase to the other in the pair. Write *bad* or *atrocious* on the line.

1. **a.** eating cold scrambled eggs _____

   b. eating cold scrambled lizard eggs with worms _____

2. **a.** weather that causes a city to become flooded _____

   b. weather that stops you from playing an outdoor game _____

Activity: Think of a bad sound, and then think of an atrocious sound. Write a paragraph or two in which you describe the sounds. Tell what makes them and what they sound like. Explain how you feel and how you might react when you hear the sounds. Include many descriptive words so the reader can picture your reaction.

_____

_____

_____

_____

_____

_____

_____

_____

_____

_____

_____

Scared, Scared, Scared

Activity: Think of all the words and phrases you can use to say or show that someone is scared. Write some of them in the box. One has been written for you.

> trembled,

Activity: Now write a story in which you use as many of these words and phrases as you can. In your story, write about something scary and explain how it could make you feel. Perhaps you see monsters, you hear loud crashing noises, or there is a natural disaster. Make it sound as if you are in the middle of the action. Then surprise your reader. Somehow reveal that you are watching a movie, listening to someone read out loud, or on an amusement park ride! Don't forget to include a title!

Slime Hunters

THINK ABOUT IT! Think of a written advertisement. Words in ads are chosen carefully. Some ads are for jobs. Businesses want people to work for them. They write ads so the most qualified people will apply.

Cueva de Villa Luz is a cave in southeastern Mexico. Scientists are needed to study the cave because it is filled with bacteria that might be similar to life on other planets. This is because the bacteria do not use energy from the sun. Instead, the bacteria combine hydrogen-sulfide gas and oxygen for energy.

Activity: Use the information above and the job facts below to write an ad for a job at Cueva de Villa Luz. Remember, you have to make the job sound appealing because you want people to apply! Use words that present the job in a positive light. Think: Will you use the word *scary* or *thrilling*?

Job Facts

- The gas will kill you, so must wear a special breathing mask.
- You will walk through white water where you can't see your feet.
- Bacteria causes walls and ceilings to drip slime.
- The smell is similar to rotten eggs.
- The acid on the walls will burn through skin and clothes, so you must wear protective gear.
- You have to squeeze through narrow passages on your hands and knees.

_____

_____

_____

_____

_____

_____

_____

_____

_____

_____

_____

_____

Cliffhanger

DID YOU KNOW? Sometimes books or TV shows are series. Often, when someone finishes one book or TV show, he or she can't wait to read or watch the next one in the series. That is because one is left wondering what will happen next. Perhaps a plane is about to crash. Perhaps a child is lost. Will people be saved? You have to read or watch more to find out!

The word *cliffhanger* is used to describe this type of ending.

Activity: Write a cliffhanger ending. It does not have to be a full story. It only has to be one paragraph, and you don't have to explain who the characters are. Start it right in the middle of the action. Just make sure that the reader wants to keep reading!

Then, below your paragraph, write some phrases or words in the box that might be used in an advertisement for the sequel. Tell when it is coming out, what it is called, and what the reader might find out.

_____

_____

_____

_____

_____

_____

_____

Nonstop Around the World

The two sentences below are both about a small cabin, but one sentence uses words that help you form a better picture in your mind. Draw a star next to that sentence.

> *The cabin was very small.*
>
> *The cabin was so cramped and tight that standing up straight was impossible and moving around was almost impossible.*

Writers use words like *cramped, tight,* and *impossible* to help readers sense or feel what is going on. The words make the writing more interesting.

Activity: Read the passage below. Then write a paragraph about what Dick and Jeana might have felt during the flight and after. Use words that help the reader feel and sense what the pilots went through on this nine-day flight.

> Dick Rutan and Jeana Yeager were the first to fly around the world without stopping. Their plane, the *Voyager*, was mostly filled with fuel. Their cabin was only 3 feet high, about 3 feet wide, and 7.5 feet long. They flew nonstop for 9 days, 3 minutes, and 44 seconds. The plane shook so violently during some storms that the pilots were badly bruised.

_____

_____

_____

_____

_____

_____

_____

_____

_____

The Same Place You Got On

Activity: Write a story with a surprise ending. Your story should include a person who gets onto a plane that has a small cabin. The person is frightened of such a small, cramped place, but thinks, "It is okay. The ride can't be that long. Since I'm getting off at the same airport where I got on, it must just be a short ride in the air." Then have the person find out that he or she is getting off where the plane takes off, but first they are flying all the way around the world!

Remember, when you write, use words that help the reader feel how small and cramped the cabin is. Tell how the person reacts or feels when he or she finds out how long the trip will take.

_____

_____

_____

_____

_____

_____

_____

_____

_____

_____

_____

_____

_____

English Lesson

THINK ABOUT IT! It is hard to learn English. For example, think of homophones. Homophones are words that sound the same, but they do not have the same meaning. They may be spelled differently, too. For example, *be* and *bee* and *hair* and *hare* are homophones.

Activity: Write a dialogue that can be used to teach English language learners about homophones. Make sure you explain what a homophone is somewhere in your dialogue and include other homophones, as well. The dialogue has been started for you.

Ted: I went to a huge sale.

Layla: What type of boat was the sail on?

Ted: I don't mean the sail on a boat! I mean _____

_____

_____

_____

_____

_____

_____

_____

_____

_____

_____

_____

_____

_____

The Right Time

Activity: Write a dialogue between a teacher and a class. The teacher is teaching the class about phobias, which are strong and intense fears; however, one student keeps interrupting. Have the student ask if the teacher has arachnophobia or xenophobia. When the teacher asks why, have the student say there is a big spider on the teacher or there is an alien at the door!

In your dialogue, make sure you say what a phobia is. Give examples of different types of phobias.

Phobia Name	Fear of
claustrophobia	closed-in spaces
arachnophobia	spiders
triskaidekaphobia	the number 13

Phobia Name	Fear of
xenophobia	strangers or aliens
acrophobia	heights
hydrophobia	water

_____
_____
_____
_____
_____
_____
_____
_____
_____
_____
_____
_____
_____

Dogs Battle Blizzard

Read the two newspaper headlines below. They both are covering the same story. What newspaper story would you rather read?

Medicine Sent for Children   OR   **Dogs Battle Blizzard to Save Children**

Writers choose words for newspaper headlines and articles that will make people want to read the stories. In the headlines above, the verbs are *sent* and *battle*. *Battle* sounds more thrilling than *sent*.

Activity: Choose one of the headlines above and write the article that goes with it. In your article, use many exciting action words to make your reader want to keep reading. Use the information in the chart below to write your story.

Who: Balto and other sled dogs   **When:** January 1925

What: Dogs ran in blizzards, strong winds, below-zero temperatures, and dense snow (so thick that a hand in front of a face could not be seen).

Where: Anchorage, Alaska, to Nome, Alaska

Why: Medicine was needed to stop deadly diphtheria outbreak nearly 1,000 miles away. The plane engine froze, so dogsledding was the only option.

By: _____

Anchorage to Nome

DID YOU KNOW?

Every year there is a race. The race celebrates the dogsled race that saved the children of Nome, Alaska in 1925. The race is called the Iditarod Trail Sled Dog Race. This race is one of the hardest and toughest in the world. The race is over 1,000 miles, going from Anchorage to Nome. It starts on the first Saturday in March. The fastest time was a little under 9 days. With wind chill, temperatures are sometimes minus 100 degrees!

Activity: Imagine that you are in this race. Write a newspaper article about your experiences. Tell *who, what, where, when,* and *why.* Use words that make the reader feel the action and the thrill. Think of ice that stabs and sinks. Think of attacking moose and cold that cuts. Make sure to include a more exciting headline than "Anchorage to Nome." You choose if you win the race or not!

_____

By: _____

_____   _____

_____   _____

_____   _____

_____   _____

_____   _____

_____   _____

_____   _____

_____   _____

_____   _____

_____   _____

Three-Circle Pig

Activity: Look at the picture. Now write a "how-to" for drawing a three-circle pig. Write steps for the circles, eyes, nostrils, ears, legs, and tail. Put the steps in the order you think they should go. For each step, explain what one should do. For example, should something be added on, in, below, or next to the outer, inner, or middle circle? Include a small illustration with each step, too.

What's Cooking?

DID YOU KNOW? Cooks are always making up new recipes. For example, it is said that the modern sandwich is named after Lord Sandwich — a British statesman who lived from 1718 to 1792. Lord Sandwich never wanted to stop playing games. He would ask his cook to give him meat between bread, and so the sandwich was born.

Activity: Make up a name and recipe for a new food. It can be a kind of sandwich, dessert, main dish, snack, drink, or a food type we have never heard of before! It can be silly or serious. Write a "how-to" for preparing your new food. Your "how-to" should include the following:

- a title
- a list of ingredients
- steps on what to add and when
- oven temperature, cooking time, campfire, etc.
- how or when the food might be served (breakfast, trail food, to keep hungry bears away, etc.)

Remember, your food can be silly or serious! You may include a drawing of what this new food looks like on a separate sheet of paper.

_____

_____

_____

_____

_____

_____

_____

_____

Splat!

Which sentence forms a better action picture in your head?

> *Splat! Splat! Splat! Water balloons were bursting everywhere!*
>
> *Water balloons were landing everywhere.*

The first sentence forms a better action picture in your head for two reasons. First, the word *splat* is a sound word. The sound helps one picture the action. Second, the verb *bursting* is more exciting than *landing*.

Activity: Write down as many sound words as you can in the box below.

Activity: Now think of a noisy time. It might be in a cafeteria, jungle, store, or mall. It might be at a game or at a factory. Describe the place or event using as many sound words from your list as you can.

_____

_____

_____

_____

_____

_____

_____

_____

Quiet Time

Activity: Think of all the words you can that mean or make you think of quiet. Write them in the box below.

Activity: Now write a story scene in which people are told to be quiet so that a relative can take a nap. Instead of quiet, there is noise, noise, noise! Perhaps the noise is because of music, an accident, an earthquake, a fire, a wild animal—you choose. Then have the relative wake up. The people are scared that they are going to get in trouble. Then, at the end, they find out that the relative couldn't hear a thing! He or she was wearing headphones or ear plugs during the nap!

Use as many sound words for *quiet* as you can in your story.

_____

_____

_____

_____

_____

_____

_____

_____

_____

_____

_____

Footwear

DID YOU KNOW? Did you know that sandals were the most common type of footwear in early civilizations? Did you know that it wasn't until the 19th century that there were left and right shoes? Before then, both shoes were identical.

Activity: Write three paragraphs about shoes using the following guide:

Paragraph 1: Tell what shoes are good for. Tell why you think sandals were common so long ago. Tell why you think left and right shoes were identical.

Paragraph 2: Describe in detail what shoes you are wearing now. Then describe what kinds of shoes you like.

Paragraph 3: Discuss shoe rules. Many places do not allow people in if they are not wearing shoes. Do you agree or disagree? Why? Tell if your school has a dress code about shoes. Do you agree, or would you change it? Why?

_____

_____

_____

_____

_____

_____

_____

_____

_____

_____

_____

_____

The First Shoes

Activity: Write a story that takes place long ago. The basic plotline is that shoes have not been invented yet. A boy or girl invents a pair of shoes. At first, all the people laugh at the child, but then something happens. The child can run faster than everyone else because his or her feet are protected, or the child is able to save others because of the shoes. Then everyone wants the child to make shoes for them.

In your story, tell how and why the child invents the shoes. Describe what the shoes look like. Use action words when you describe when and how the child runs faster or saves others. Don't forget to include a title!

Title:

_____

_____

_____

_____

_____

_____

_____

_____

_____

_____

_____

_____

_____

Like a Roller Coaster

IMAGINE THAT!

Go on a roller coaster, and you will probably be in for a wild ride. On a roller coaster, you may go slow and up, and then fast and down. You may drop quickly, go backward, or even go upside down. You may be terrified, filled with excitement, or even feel sick! Once the ride starts, you can't get off.

Activity: Write a paragraph in which you compare your life to a roller coaster. Your topic sentence should say who you are and how your life can be compared to a roller coaster. Then give examples of how, just like a roller coaster, your life has had fast and slow times. Describe times when you felt you were going down, up, and backward. Tell about a time when you felt scared, excited, or like you were trapped inside a car while hanging upside down!

_____

_____

_____

_____

_____

_____

_____

_____

_____

_____

_____

_____

Stubborn as a Mule

THINK ABOUT IT! A writer might say someone is as stubborn as a mule. Most likely, who would the writer say this about?

    a. someone who always changes his or her mind

    b. someone who never changes his or her mind

Activity: Make up a person and use what you know about animals to compare the person to four different animals. Use the words *as a* when you make your comparison. Then add two or three sentences that help form a picture in the reader's mind.

> **Example:** *Sally is as stubborn as a mule. One time she said she would only sit in the front seat. When an enormous crocodile got on the bus, Sally refused to get off. She told the crocodile that she wouldn't give up her seat for anybody or anything!*

1. _____

_____

_____

_____

2. _____

_____

_____

_____

3. _____

_____

_____

_____

4. _____

_____

_____

_____

Yellowstone

Writers choose their words wisely when they want to show action. Read the two sentences below. Which sentence makes one feel more action?

My heart pounded, banging my ribs, as I stared in astonishment.

I had never seen such a thing before.

In the first sentence, the reader can picture and feel what is going on. The second sentence is just a statement that tells the reader something without showing any action.

DID YOU KNOW?

John Colter explored Yellowstone in 1807. It is believed that he was the first person of European descent to see it. Colter came back with tales of bubbling mud pots, steaming pools of water, and geysers. No one believed Colter. In fact, people made fun of him!

Activity: Write two diary entries for Colter. In your entries, use action words to describe what Colter felt and saw. Include adventures involving hot springs, geysers, or wild animals. Think about the weather when you pick your month. Be sure to write the date for each entry.

Moon Trip

Writers choose their words wisely when they want to show action. Read the two sentences below. Which sentence makes one feel more action?

> *I went over the rock.*
>
> *I leaped high into the air and safely over the jagged rock.*

In the first sentence, the writer tells the reader something without showing any action. In the second sentence, the reader can picture exactly what happened.

Activity: Imagine that you found a way to go to the moon. Record two diary entries about your adventures there. Be as creative as you want with your adventures. Be sure to include many action words so the entries are exciting to read.

Remember, when you are on the moon, you weigh one-sixth of what you do now. You can jump about six times higher!

Letter to a Sister City

Word Choice

DID YOU KNOW? There are some cities that are "sister cities." Sister cities are two cities in two different places. They may be in different states or countries. The two cities make agreements to promote cultural and business connections.

Activity: Write a letter that could be sent to a student from a sister city of your choice. In your letter, describe some things about your school and culture. (Your culture is your way of life, which includes the foods you eat, how you dress, and what you do for fun.) Explain at least one slang word or phrase, too. For example, a visitor might not know that "Way to go!" can mean, "You did a good job."

Dear _____ ,

_____

_____

_____

_____

_____

_____

_____

_____

_____

_____

_____

                        _____

Letter to a Friend

THINK ABOUT IT! When you write a letter to a friend, you do not have to be formal. You can use slang words or informal language. You can use as many abbreviations (LOL and BFF, for example) as you like.

Activity: Write a one-paragraph letter to your friend. Use as many slang words and expressions as you can. Then rewrite the letter so that someone who is unfamiliar with these slang words could understand it. Think: If you say, "We left so we wouldn't get kicked out," does it mean one would be kicked by someone's foot?

Dear _____ ,

_____

_____

_____

_____

                                    _____

Dear _____ ,

_____

_____

_____

_____

                                    _____

Helen Keller

DID YOU KNOW? Helen Keller became blind and deaf before she turned two. With the help of her teacher Annie Sullivan, Helen learned to "talk" by signing. To "hear," she would feel the signs that other people made with their hands.

At first, Helen did not know what the signs meant. Then, one day, Annie spelled *w-a-t-e-r* over and over while she pumped water onto Helen's hand. It was then that Helen realized that things had names. Different signs stood for different names!

Activity: Now think about colors. How would you describe colors to someone who cannot see? Write two sentences about each color below. Try to match each color with a smell, a feeling, and something you can touch. Give examples of things that have that color. For example, if no one had told her, Helen might have thought that some people had orange-colored eyes or green skin.

Red: _____

_____

_____

Orange: _____

_____

_____

Yellow: _____

_____

_____

Green: _____

_____

_____

Blue: _____

_____

_____

Purple: _____

_____

_____

Morning Surprise

IMAGINE THAT!

Imagine that you or a fictional character has awakened and turned a bright primary color! (The primary colors are red, blue, and yellow.)

Activity: Describe how people react and what happens. Do you or the character ever look "normal" again? Don't forget to include a title!

Title:

_____

_____

_____

_____

_____

_____

_____

_____

_____

_____

_____

_____

_____

_____

_____

Animal Cross Poem

Activity: Think of two real animals, and then combine them into one. Write a poem about your "animal cross" (one animal made from two others). Your poem can be long or short and can rhyme or not rhyme. Be sure to use good clue words to describe your new animal. Say the name of your animal cross at the beginning or end of your poem. Then write a second animal cross poem using two other real animals. See the example below, which combines a dog and an octopus.

Dogopus

Good thing it has eight legs,

Instead of eight heads.

This means it barks once

For every eight balls it catches!

Dogopus

Fluency

Sensational Superstar

Read the phrases below. What is common about each one?

slippery snake   **crazy cat**   **fast and furious**   **safe and sound**   **wacky walrus**

In the phrases above, the sound in the first syllables is repeated. All of these phrases are alliterative. Alliteration is when the beginning consonant sounds of consecutive words are repeated.

Sometimes writers will use alliteration to make their writing more playful. The repeating sounds make their writing fun to say. It helps it flow.

Activity: Write a paragraph about yourself using as many alliterative phrases and expressions as you can. Be creative! For example, don't just say you like pizza. Say you like pizza pieces or pizza pies. Don't just say you have a pet. Say you have a precious, pretty, priceless pet. Start by calling yourself a sensational superstar.

_____

_____

_____

_____

_____

_____

_____

_____

_____

_____

_____

_____

Funny Fiction Folk

THINK ABOUT IT! Alliteration is when the beginning consonant sounds of consecutive words are repeated. For example, "The big, bad, worthless wolf snickered and smacked his mushy mouth at the pretty, porky pig."

Activity: Think of a folk tale, moral, or children's story. Rewrite or retell part of the story using as much alliteration as you can.

Story Ideas

The Tortoise and the Hare

Goldilocks and the Three Bears

The Ugly Duckling

The Three Little Pigs

The Boy Who Cried Wolf

Little Red Riding Hood

_____

_____

_____

_____

_____

_____

_____

_____

_____

_____

_____

_____

DID YOU KNOW?

Frogs are amphibians. They range in size from 3/8 of an inch to 13.5 inches long. Frogs are either dully or brightly colored. The dull ones rely on camouflage for protection. The bright ones are often small, but their skin secretes poison. The frogs' bright colors ward off predators. Some frog poison is strong enough to kill people.

By eating insects, spiders, worms, and slugs, frogs help control pest populations. The biggest frogs will sometimes eat mice!

Both male and female frogs care for their offspring. Some male frogs will carry tadpoles to the water on their backs. Some female frogs will eat the eggs and then vomit them up when they are tadpoles!

Activity: How do you feel about frogs? Some people eat frogs. Other people enjoy the sound they make. Some people find frogs to be horrible, while others find them fascinating. Write down all the words one might use to describe frogs and how one might feel about them.

Likes frogs: <u>fascinating,</u>

Does not like frogs: <u>horrible,</u>

Activity: Write two paragraphs in which you explain how you feel about frogs. Tell why others might feel the opposite and why. When you write, use words from your lists above. Include frog facts in your paragraph, too.

_____

_____

_____

_____

_____

_____

_____

_____

_____

The Small Pet

Activity: Write a short story or a scene from a story with this basic plotline: a child pesters his or her parent for a pet frog. The child names some advantages about frogs. The parent finally says yes if it is small. The child comes home from a nearby pond with a small frog. Tell how the parent feels and reacts before and after he or she finds out that the frog is brightly colored and may be poisonous! Write at least two paragraphs and add a title.

Title:

_____

_____

_____

_____

_____

_____

_____

_____

_____

_____

_____

_____

_____

_____

_____

_____

_____

The Great Pyramids

When you write, you need to make sure your story makes sense. Why doesn't the story below make sense? (Hint: Two things don't make sense.)

> *I sailed down the Amazon River in Brazil with my family. We visited the Great Pyramids. The pyramids were amazing. They were built as burial tombs for the pharaohs, or kings. The pharaohs were made into mummies and buried inside the pyramids. One mummy said he was King Tut. King Tut was only nine or ten years old when he became king!*

In the story, it sounds as if the Great Pyramids are in Brazil instead of Egypt. Also, because of the way it is worded, it sounds as if the mummy is talking!

How could you fix this story so it makes sense?

1. _____

2. _____

Activity: Write about a place that you visited or about something you did. Include two things in your story that do not make sense. For example, it might seem that you are in a different place or time than the one you are talking about, or it might seem as if an animal or nonliving thing is actually talking. Show or read your paragraph to your classmates. Could anyone tell what didn't make sense?

_____

_____

_____

_____

_____

_____

_____

_____

Danger at Night

When you write, you need to make sure your story makes sense. Why doesn't the story below make sense? (Hint: Two things don't make sense.)

It was so dark that I couldn't see my hands. I was scared, but I knew I had to go on. I walked carefully, feeling the rocky ground before I put my feet down. Then I heard the most horrible sound. It was close behind me! I turned, and by the bright light of the moon, I saw it! It was a hungry ogre! I tried to stay on my horse's back, but he was bucking too wildly.

Is it very dark or not? Is the person walking or not?

How could you fix this story so it makes sense?

1. _____

2. _____

Activity: Make up a story or describe something with at least one thing not making sense. It may have to do with the wrong season or time. It may have to do with something that doesn't fit or work. Use your imagination! When you are done, share your story with your classmates. Could anyone tell what didn't make sense?

_____

_____

_____

_____

_____

_____

_____

Cockroach, Cockroach

Words can help set a mood in writing. Read each phrase about cockroaches below and write "interesting" or "disgusting" before each one to describe its mood.

☐	*To think they lived with dinosaurs!*
☐	*Gross, ancient beasts of dirt and damp*
☐	*Crawly, filthy, yucky*
☐	*Six legs and 18 knees or more*
☐	*Brave traveler, hitching a ride to America on wooden ships*
☐	*A sad day, this spread of white-blooded pests*
☐	*Cut off the head, and the terror doesn't end*
☐	*Thrilling that it can live a month without a head!*

The words in the lines above help set a mood. They match how the writer wants us to feel. The words *gross, crawly, filthy, yucky, pests*, and *terror* make us feel disgust. They don't make us feel good about cockroaches. Though some may not like cockroaches, words like *brave* and *thrilling* help us to view them in a different light.

Activity: Now it's your turn. Write two mood poems. First, choose any living thing. Then think of it in both a negative and a positive light. Write six or more lines in each poem. The lines can be factual, or they can be about how you feel. Your lines can be a mix of complete sentences, phrases, and lists of words. The lines need to set a mood and help the reader know how you feel. Read your poems out loud to your classmates. Could they tell which poem set a positive or negative mood?

Mood: Positive	Mood: Negative
_____	_____
_____	_____
_____	_____
_____	_____
_____	_____
_____	_____

Little Miss Muffet

The nursery rhyme about Miss Muffet goes like this:

Little Miss Muffet sat on a tuffet

Eating her curds and whey

Along came a spider,

Who sat down beside her

And frightened Miss Muffet away.

Activity: Write two mood poems. In the first poem, have Miss Muffet describe the spider, how she feels about it, and what happened. In the second poem, have the spider describe Miss Muffet. Your poems should have at least seven lines each. They can be a mix of sentences, phrases, and individual words. The words you choose should set a mood. They should let the reader see how Miss Muffet and the spider view the same event differently.

The Top of Everest

THINK ABOUT IT! When you write, you do not want all of your sentences to be the same. You want to have a variety of long and short ones. This helps your writing flow, and it keeps your writing interesting. One way to combine two sentences into one is shown below.

> *Erik is a climber. He reached the top of Mount Everest.*
>
> *Erik, a climber, reached the top of Mount Everest.*

Activity: Combine the two sentences into one long one in the same way as the example above. Be sure to include commas.

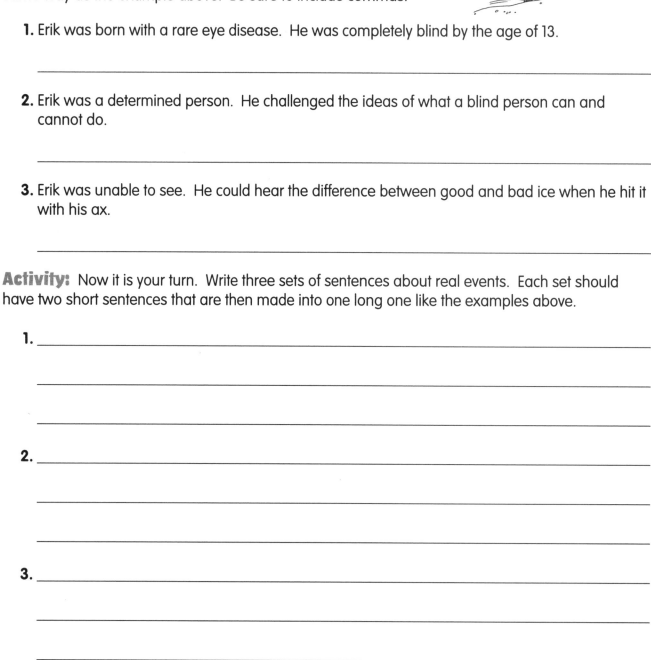

1. Erik was born with a rare eye disease. He was completely blind by the age of 13.

   _____

2. Erik was a determined person. He challenged the ideas of what a blind person can and cannot do.

   _____

3. Erik was unable to see. He could hear the difference between good and bad ice when he hit it with his ax.

   _____

Activity: Now it is your turn. Write three sets of sentences about real events. Each set should have two short sentences that are then made into one long one like the examples above.

1. _____

   _____

   _____

2. _____

   _____

   _____

3. _____

   _____

   _____

Climbing News

IMAGINE THAT!

Imagine that you are a reporter. You are telling the story of Erik Weihenmayer, the blind climber who reached the top of Mount Everest.

Activity: Write down what you will say. Vary your sentences by having long and short ones. This will make the news easier to listen to. It also helps people pay attention. Use descriptive words that excite the reader, too. Then say your newscast out loud. Did the different kinds of sentences help it flow?

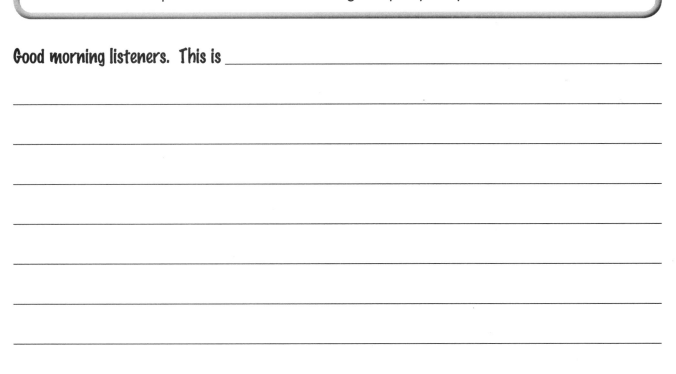

Event Facts

- May 25, 2001, Erik Weihenmayer reaches top of Everest
- world's highest mountain in the Himalayas
- brutal, cold, savage winds
- not enough air at top to survive for long
- listened to bells on other climbers
- would listen to "thunk" of his ax on ice—could tell good ice from bad ice
- can hear the sound of open space compared to closed space due to sound vibrations
- said about drop-offs—"It's an overwhelming and pretty scary sound."

Good morning listeners. This is _____

_____

_____

_____

_____

_____

_____

_____

_____

_____

Brushing Lesson

Fluency

THINK ABOUT IT!

When we talk, we do not talk to all people the same way. For example, we may use slang when we talk to our friends. When we talk to babies, we repeat words and use simple sentences.

Activity: Write a dialogue in which you are teaching a child of preschool age how to properly brush his or her teeth. Think about how to phrase and order your information. Remember that children of this age often ask, "Why?"

_____

_____

_____

_____

_____

_____

_____

_____

_____

_____

_____

_____

_____

_____

_____

_____

Pet Talk

Activity: Write an imaginary dialogue between two animals. One animal is an old pet that has lived with a family for many years. The old pet is explaining things to the other animal, a new pet, about the people with whom they both live. When you write, do not have the animals refer to themselves as pets. Have them describe the people as if the humans were the pets!

You can choose the kind of animals and give them names. What do the animals think about their "pets" and how the humans look and behave? Use your imagination!

State Borders

Fluency

THINK ABOUT IT!

Where is your state located? You can say where things are located in more than one way. Changing your sentences helps keep your writing from being the same. It helps the reader stay interested.

Example: *What state, states, country, or body of water borders your state to the west?*

Example answers:

- *Texas, my state, is bordered to the west by New Mexico.*
- *My state is Texas, and it is bordered to the west by New Mexico.*
- *New Mexico is west of my state, Texas.*

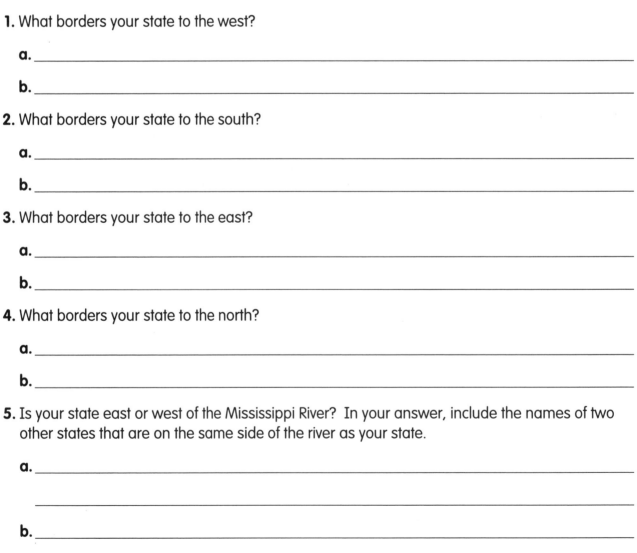

TEXAS

Activity: Now it is your turn. Practice writing different sentences by answering each question in **two** different ways.

1. What borders your state to the west?

    a. _____

    b. _____

2. What borders your state to the south?

    a. _____

    b. _____

3. What borders your state to the east?

    a. _____

    b. _____

4. What borders your state to the north?

    a. _____

    b. _____

5. Is your state east or west of the Mississippi River? In your answer, include the names of two other states that are on the same side of the river as your state.

    a. _____

    _____

    b. _____

    _____

Take Your Seat

Fluency

DID YOU KNOW? It is thought that the head of the table is the most powerful seat. For that reason, presidents from different countries will often meet at a round table. This way, no one country seems more powerful than the other.

Activity: Imagine that your president is meeting with seven other world leaders. Your job is to make a seating chart for all eight country leaders. Think of seven other countries besides your own. Decide who will be sitting where. Then describe where **five** of the countries will be placed in at least two different ways. Plan ahead! Write in the names of where each country's representative will be seated in the pie chart to the right.

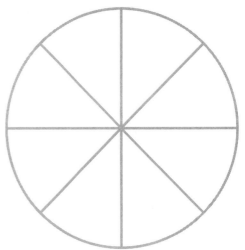

For example:

   a. Russia will be to the left of the United States.

   b. To the left of the United States is Russia, which is directly across from Canada.

1. a. _____

   b. _____

2. a. _____

   b. _____

3. a. _____

   b. _____

4. a. _____

   b. _____

5. a. _____

   b. _____

If someone only read your sentences, do you think he or she would come up with the same seating chart you made? _____

Stopped Trains

Activity: Using the facts from the box below, write a newspaper article about what stopped the trains in Victoria, Australia. Tell *what, where, when,* and *why*. Make sure your sentences flow. Use words that make the reader feel excited and astonished. End with a comment about the following question: What if the Portuguese millipedes had never come to Australia?

Portuguese Millipedes Fact Box

- Victoria, Australia
- April 2002
- Trains were forced to a halt over 50 times in one month.
- Train wheels couldn't get traction because of oily goo on tracks.
- Oily goo comes from squashed Portuguese millipedes.
- Each millipede is less than 2 inches long, but there were tons of them!
- They were accidentally introduced into Australia in the 1950s.
- They have no natural enemies because their taste is so bad.

_____

_____

_____

_____

_____

_____

_____

_____

_____

_____

_____

_____

Slip and Slide

Activity: Write a fictional newspaper article about a day all the students at your school were late. Why was everyone tardy? They were busy slipping and sliding on squashed insects! Make up a name for the kind of insect and explain why it caused children to slip and slide. Tell where and when this happened, and include fun and exciting details. You can make your story silly or scary, but make sure no one gets hurt. End with a comment about these questions: What if there had not been any insects? Would every child have been tardy?

Review your story when you are done. Verify that your sentences flow smoothly.

By: _____

_____

Invitation to Speak

Activity: Sometimes guest speakers come to classrooms to talk about their lives, their jobs, or to inform others about a topic. Think of someone alive that you would like to be a guest speaker at your school. The person can be famous or working at a place you want to know more about. Write a letter to the person asking him or her to come speak in your classroom.

Remember, you want your letter to stand out. Write it so that it sounds so important and fun that the speaker will definitely want to come to your class. First, introduce yourself and your class. Then tell why the person would be a good speaker for the class. Tell when and where he or she could speak and on what topic. Add a personal note about why it would mean a lot to you, other students, and the community.

Dear _____ ,

_____

_____

_____

_____

_____

_____

_____

_____

_____

_____

_____

So Sorry

THINK ABOUT IT!

Sometimes we need to apologize. We may need to apologize even if we could not stop the event that happened.

Activity: Write a letter to a friend in which you apologize for not meeting him or her like you said you would. In your letter, tell what led to the missed meeting. Before you write, plan ahead by thinking of a chain of events in which one thing leads to another. Your chain of events can be lifelike or wild and crazy. You should have at least four events in your chain. Have fun planning what leads to what! (Note: You can have as many events in your chain reaction as you want.)

Planning Example: (Event 1) Shoelace came untied, (Event 2) Tripped on a lace and fell into a hole, (Event 3) Landed on the opposite side of Earth!, (Event 4) Had to fly in a jet to get back home. Result = missed meeting friend

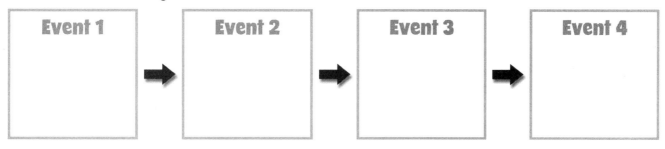

| Event 1 | Event 2 | Event 3 | Event 4 |

Dear _____,

_____

_____

_____

_____

_____

_____

_____

                                    _____

School Directions

Activity: You have a substitute teacher who doesn't know his or her way around the school. The substitute asks you to write directions. Tell the substitute how to get from your classroom to the principal's office.

Title your directions and record them as steps. Use directional words such as *left*, *right*, *after*, *before*, *up*, and *down*. Describe what rooms or objects he or she will pass. Will mentioning colors or floor coverings help make the directions clear? If it is very easy to get to the principal's office, then give directions from your classroom to the library, cafeteria, or another teacher's classroom.

Treasure Hunt

IMAGINE THAT!

Imagine that you are setting up a treasure hunt at school. There are five stops on the treasure hunt.

Activity: Provide clues and directions for each stop, using words such as *left, right, after, before, across, up,* and *down.* Think about how to describe things without making it too easy for the reader. For example, don't say, "The next clue is at the bottom of the slide." Instead say, "The next clue is located to the right of the swing set and to the left of the monkey bars. It is right under where you land when going down!"

Before you start, plan your hunt. Choose the location of each stop. Plan what the treasure is, too.

Stop 1 (start)	Stop 2	Stop 3	Stop 4	Stop 5 (end)

Treasure =

Now record the instructions and/or clues for each stop. Stop 5 does not need a clue, but it needs a note to the treasure hunter about the treasure.

Stop 1: _____

_____

Stop 2: _____

_____

Stop 3: _____

_____

Stop 4: _____

_____

Stop 5: _____

_____

Hot or Cold

DID YOU KNOW?

There is a game in which you think of something in a room. As the "it" person looks for the object, you give clues by saying, "warm, warmer, hot, hotter, cold, colder, etc." *Warm* means that the person is getting close to the object. *Hot* means that the person is very close to the object. *Cold* means that the person is far from the object. The "hotter" the person is, the closer he or she is to finding the object.

Activity: What if you were playing this game? Choose an object in the classroom. Think about where it is. Provide hints for where it is located. Use each of the following words at least one time when you write your hints: *above, below, left, right, after, before, by, next to*. Make sure you write a comment with your directions, too.

> **Example:** *If you think the object is the clock on the front wall **above** the chalkboard, you are freezing! You may as well be in Antarctica!*

Freezing: _____

_____

Cold: _____

_____

Chilly: _____

_____

Warm: _____

_____

Hot: _____

_____

Burning: _____

_____

Have your classmates read your sentences. Could they guess what object you had in mind?

Too Hot

Fluency

Activity: Think of a name for a boy or girl. Then write a paragraph in which this person talks about the sun rising. Have the person describe how the sun moves and how it gets higher in the sky. Tell how the person feels as he or she goes from freezing to cold to chilly to warm to burning. Include many descriptive words and adjectives, such as *perfect*, *delightful*, *wonderful*, *horrible*, and *mean*. Use descriptive sounds, such as *aagggh!* and *drip*, *drip*.

At the end, tell that the person has nothing left to say. All that is left is a puddle of water because the person was actually a snowman!

_____

_____

_____

_____

_____

_____

_____

_____

_____

_____

_____

_____

_____

_____

_____

Circus Barker

DID YOU KNOW?

A circus barker is a person. This is the person who stands outside and tries to get people to buy tickets. The barker must be fluent. When he talks, he can't stop and pause. His sentences can't all sound the same. He must make people pay attention because he wants them to pay for a ticket!

Activity: Write down in two paragraphs what a circus barker might say. Plan ahead. Think about what attractions a circus has. What should the barker say about them that will catch people's interest? How can he say it so that people will pay attention and want to buy tickets? Plan ahead using the boxes below. What will the barker mention?

Animals	Games	Shows

_____

_____

_____

_____

_____

_____

_____

_____

_____

_____

Magic Trick

Fluency

THINK ABOUT IT! Magicians are not silent. In fact, they talk a lot! Their talk makes you pay attention. It keeps you focused on what the magician wants you to notice. Magicians spend a lot of time setting up tricks and making the audience expect something.

Activity: Imagine you are a magician in a circus. Write down what you will say as you perform the following magic trick:

1. Ask for a volunteer. Find out his (or her) name. For example, it might be Carlos.

2. Somehow, get Carlos to write his name on a piece of paper. You decide how it will get written.

3. Say you will put Carlos through a key ring. Make sure the audience knows the ring can't expand or get bigger.

4. Put the piece of the paper that has the written name of Carlos through the ring!

5. Tell the audience that you put Carlos through the key ring!

When you write, think about the whole trick. Think how at first the audience will be expecting one thing. Think about how, at the end, they will be laughing at themselves. Be careful with your words, and make sure you are always telling the truth!

_____

_____

_____

_____

_____

_____

_____

_____

_____

_____

Apollo

DID YOU KNOW?

Apollo is an ancient Greek god. He was the god of the sun. People believed that, every day, Apollo drove his chariot of fiery horses across the sky to give light to the world.

Today we know that the sun does not move across the sky. The Earth turns, and so it only looks as though the sun is moving.

Activity: Even though we know the facts, it is still fun to make up fiction. Write a paragraph or two in which you make up a story that explains a natural event. The natural event may be a planet, moon, or sun movement. It may be earthquakes, volcanoes, seasons, or the tides. You choose!

When you write, first make up an ancient god or goddess. Describe the god or goddess and what he or she does. Then explain what the god does to explain the natural event. Don't forget to include a title!

Title:

_____

_____

_____

_____

_____

_____

_____

_____

_____

_____

_____

_____

Voice

Golf

Activity: Write two paragraphs about the sport of golf. In the first paragraph, tell what you think the basic goal of the game is and what equipment one might use. Describe where people play. Are there any golf courses close to you? Do you know anyone famous or not so famous who plays golf?

In the second paragraph, tell how you personally feel about golf. Tell if you have ever played golf, and whether you would like to play more or learn how to play. Explain if you think the land for golf courses is being put to good use. Also, tell if you would rather play or watch another sport and why.

_____

_____

_____

_____

_____

_____

_____

_____

_____

_____

_____

_____

_____

The King and Golf

Voice

DID YOU KNOW?

Long ago, a king banned golf. When something is banned, it is not allowed. King James II of Scotland banned the game in 1457. Why did he ban golf? At that time, people fought and hunted with bows and arrows. The king felt that golf distracted young men from archery practice! King James II wasn't the only king who felt this way. King James the III and IV also banned the game. The ban wasn't lifted until 1502.

Activity: Imagine that you are King James II of Scotland. Write a paragraph in which you describe how you feel about the game of golf. Explain why you banned the game and how you think the ban is good for people and the country. Start your paragraph with, "I am King James II of Scotland."

Next, imagine that you are a subject of King James II in 1457. How do you think you would feel about the golf ban? Write a second paragraph in which you explain why the ban is fair or unfair. Start your paragraph with, "I am _____ , a subject of King James II."

_____

_____

_____

_____

_____

_____

_____

_____

_____

_____

_____

_____

North on Top

Voice

THINK ABOUT IT!

Look on a map. Where is north? It is always at the top. East is to the right. Why? Long ago there was an astronomer from Egypt. He lived almost 2,000 years ago. His name was Ptolemy. Ptolemy put north to the top and east to the right. Mapmakers followed Ptolemy. Perhaps this was because most of the known countries were in the north.

Activity: It doesn't have to be this way! It is just the custom. Think about how people from Australia might feel. They are told they live at the bottom of the world. Write an essay with your view. Outline your writing below and write your paragraphs on another sheet of paper.

Paragraph 1: Tell how maps are drawn and how they came to be.

Paragraph 2: Tell how someone from the Southern Hemisphere might have a different perspective. How would you feel if you were told you lived at the bottom of the world?

Paragraph 3: Tell why all, some, or no maps should be drawn with south at the top. Are there advantages to maps being drawn the same?

_____

_____

_____

_____

_____

_____

_____

_____

_____

_____

_____

_____

The Strange Map

IMAGINE THAT!

Imagine you are in Australia. You are looking at a map. At first, the map looks very strange. You recognize the country names, but something looks wrong. Then you understand! The map has south at the top! The North Pole is not at the top of the world. It is at the bottom of the world! All the countries look upside down!

Activity: Write a letter to a friend telling him or her about the map. Describe how the map looked and how it made you feel. Tell if you think it is a good map. Give four examples of what countries and/or states are on top of or below each other. For example, "It was so strange to see Canada below the United States instead of above it!"

Dear _____,

_____

_____

_____

_____

_____

_____

_____

_____

_____

                                                    _____

Money

Activity: Write two paragraphs about money. In the first paragraph, tell what kinds of money are used in your country. Describe the coins and bills. Then tell who makes the money and where it is made.

In the second paragraph, tell why people use money. Give two examples in your own life when you (or someone you know) used money. How did money make the transaction (the buying and selling) easier?

Money Talk

Voice

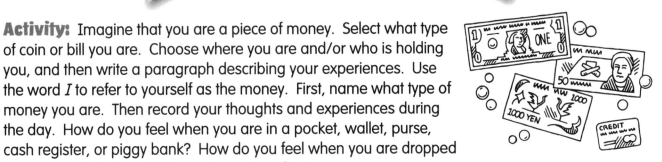

Activity: Imagine that you are a piece of money. Select what type of coin or bill you are. Choose where you are and/or who is holding you, and then write a paragraph describing your experiences. Use the word *I* to refer to yourself as the money. First, name what type of money you are. Then record your thoughts and experiences during the day. How do you feel when you are in a pocket, wallet, purse, cash register, or piggy bank? How do you feel when you are dropped or are in a dark place? Where do you travel to?

Include a lot of emotion in your story. You can, as the money, complain or be excited about all that happens to you.

_____

_____

_____

_____

_____

_____

_____

_____

_____

_____

_____

_____

Bike-Ride Lesson

Activity: Write two diary entries. One entry will be written before you learned how to ride a bike. The second entry will be written after you learned. (If you prefer, you can write about learning how to do something else.)

In the first entry, tell how it feels to not know how to do something. How will you learn? Why do you want to learn? Are you nervous? What might happen? Will it be worth the work and effort?

In the second entry, tell how you feel now that you can do it. Was it harder or easier than you expected? What adventures can you have now? Do you have any words of advice for new learners?

_____

_____

_____

_____

_____

_____

_____

_____

_____

_____

_____

_____

Mystery Dogs

DID YOU KNOW?

Horses are not native to the Americas. Spanish explorers brought them to the New World, or the Americas, in the early 1500s. Some Native Americans called horses *mystery dogs*. One man said, "Their dogs are great monsters with flat ears and long tongues which hang out."

Horses were soon tamed and used by many Native Americans. Using horses meant they could travel farther, carry larger loads, and hunt with more speed.

Activity: Write two diary entries for a Native American. One entry should be about seeing his or her first horse. The second entry should be written ten years later. Include a lot of descriptive words and feelings in your entries. Write using the word *I* because you are writing from the perspective of the Native American.

Date _____ : _____

_____

_____

_____

_____

_____

_____

Date _____ : _____

_____

_____

_____

_____

_____

Space Message

Voice

DID YOU KNOW?

In 1977, two messages were sent into space on the *Voyager* spacecrafts. The messages were on golden records. The messages were for extraterrestrials, or life on other planets. The records had 116 images as well as sounds that scientists felt showed life on Earth. Some of the images were diagrams while others were pictures. Some of the sounds were of insects, birds, and whales. There were greetings in 55 different languages.

Activity: What if you could send a message into space? What three images would you send? What three sounds would you send? (For example, you could send someone playing a song, someone talking, or natural sounds.) Describe in detail each of the images and sounds and tell why you chose them.

Shooting-Star Message

Voice

IMAGINE THAT!

Imagine that you see a very bright shooting star. The next day, you happen to find a strange bottle in the same area where you saw the shooting star. You open up the bottle, and a three-dimensional image pops out! It is a message from someone in a faraway galaxy!

Activity: Write two paragraphs about finding the bottle, how you felt when you saw the message, and what the message said. Then tell what you do. Do you meet an extraterrestrial? Do you tell scientists about what you find? Do you have an adventure?

Feelings About Spinach

DID YOU KNOW? A cinquain is a five-line poem about a noun. (You say it *sing-cane.*) A noun is the name of a person, place, thing, or idea. Cinquain poems have five lines and are usually unrhymed.

Activity: Choose a subject or thing that you are interested in. It can be a game, an animal, or anything you want. Remember, you must like or be interested in the subject! Then write two cinquain poems about it following the guide below. The first poem should show your true feelings. The second poem should be written with a different perspective. It should be written by someone who doesn't like the subject. See the examples below.

Title (same as line 1)

Line 1: one word for the topic (subject or noun)

Line 2: two words that describe your topic (adjectives)

Line 3: three action words that end with -ing (verbs)

Line 4: four words that describe feelings related to your topic

Line 5: one word that sums up or is a synonym for line 1

Example 1

Spinach

Spinach
Delicious, healthy
Growing, picking, eating
Can't wait to swallow!
Vegetable

Example 2

Spinach

Spinach
Horrible, leafy
Squirming, cringing, crying
Must I swallow it?
Help!

_____

_____

_____

_____

_____

_____

_____

_____

_____

_____

You and the Fly

Activity: You are most definitely not a fly. You and a fly like and dislike things for very different reasons. Write two haiku poems. The poems will be about the same subject, but they will be written from different perspectives. One poem will be from your perspective. The other will be from the fly's perspective!

A haiku poem has three short lines and paints a mental image in the reader's mind. Usually, the syllable count for the lines is 5, 7, and 5. For your poems, focus on the mental image, or picture. Don't worry if you have one or two extra or missing syllables.

Your subject can be any type of food, animal, place, or even a season. It could be the wind, a ballpark, a garbage can, a screen, a flyswatter, a ceiling, or anything you want. See the examples below.

Dog (a person's perspective)

A furry-tailed beast

Wagging tail a cheerful flag

A wordless best friend

Dog (a fly's perspective)

Leaves food in his dish

Great place to lay lots of eggs

Such a helpful beast!

Read your poems to the class. Could other students tell if the poem was written from your perspective or the fly's?

Funny Riddles

THINK ABOUT IT! Riddles are supposed to be funny. Sometimes people do not find riddles funny. This is because they don't understand them.

Activity: Write a dialogue between you and another person. In your dialogue, explain to the person why two or more of the following riddles are funny.

Q: What did one penny say to the other penny? **A:** Let's get together and make some sense.

Q: When is an ocean friendly? **A:** When it waves.

Q: What did the math book say to the doctor? **A:** I have lots of problems.

Q: How do you make the word *one* disappear? **A:** Put a *g* in front of it, and it's *gone*!

_____

_____

_____

_____

_____

_____

_____

_____

_____

_____

_____

_____

_____

_____

_____

Who Is Talking?

Activity: Think of a kind of animal. Then write a dialogue between two of that same kind of animal. Do not say what kind of animal it is until the end. To keep it a secret, just use two names. In your dialogue, the animals should be comparing themselves to people.

Finally, at the end, have one of them say something like, "Oh, I'm so glad I'm a _____ instead of one of those silly-looking humans!"

Example dialogue:

Sam: *Those poor humans. They only have two legs!*

Pam: *No wonder they are so slow! We can go so much faster!*

_____

_____

_____

_____

_____

_____

_____

_____

_____

_____

_____

_____

_____

Fable Review

Activity: Read the fable in the box below. A fable is a story with a moral or lesson. Then write a two-paragraph review of the fable. A review is a summary and opinion piece. Reviews are printed in newspapers, magazines, and on the Internet. Sometimes they are read out loud on the radio. A review should have a title and a byline (author's name).

First paragraph: Tell what you are reviewing by summarizing the story. Explain the moral or lesson that can be learned from this story.

Second paragraph: Did you personally like the story? Was it worth reading? What age group or who might enjoy this story most? How can the moral apply to your own life?

The Town Mouse and the Country Mouse

Once upon a time, a town mouse visited a country mouse. The town mouse laughed at the simple country foods and small cottage of the country mouse. The town mouse then invited the country mouse to the city. In the city, the two mice ate fine food in a fancy house, but they had to run to safety when cats, dogs, and people showed up. The country mouse left. He said, "I would rather eat and live simply and be safe."

_____

_____

_____

_____

_____

_____

_____

_____

_____

_____

_____

Town Living Is Better

Read the fable below about the town and country mice.

The Town Mouse and the Country Mouse

Once upon a time, a town mouse visited a country mouse. The town mouse laughed at the simple country foods and small cottage of the country mouse. The town mouse then invited the country mouse to the city. In the city, the two mice ate fine food in a fancy house, but they had to run to safety when cats, dogs, and people showed up. The country mouse left. He said, "I would rather eat and live simply and be safe."

Activity: Rewrite the story from the perspective of the town mouse so that the lesson learned is that it is better to live in the city than the country.

Before you start to write, think about how you can make the country seem as if it is not a good place to live. Use your imagination and what you know about city and country living. Think about living in a dirty, unheated hole in the ground. Consider the threat of cats, hawks, eagles, and snakes. It is your story, so you can have anything happen in any location.

_____

_____

_____

_____

_____

_____

_____

_____

_____

_____

_____

Dibs on That!

DID YOU KNOW? A company was selling a dessert. The dessert was small bits of ice cream coated with chocolate. It was called *Snack-a-Bites*, and no one was buying it. The company paid a marketing company to come up with a new name. The marketing company thought of the expression, "I've got dibs on that." They changed the name from *Snack-a-Bites* to *Dibs*. What happened? Lots of people bought *Dibs*, and the product became a hit!

Activity: Think of a product that kids your age do not think is popular or cool and would not be their first choice. It could be carrot juice, mouthwash, soap, a toy, or anything else you choose. Then make up a new name for it so that it will become a more popular item.

Write a short paragraph in which you tell why you think the new name will work better for the product among kids your age. Then write an ad for the product with the new name. Use words that will make people want to buy the product. Your ad can be a basic picture with words, or it can be a written paragraph.

Grandparent Bike

IMAGINE THAT!

You probably do not want the same bike that your grandparents would want. They would most likely want different bike features than you. Imagine that you made a bike that is perfect for grandparents.

Activity: Write a short paragraph in which you describe what the name of your bike is and why the name will help the bike sell. List some of the bike's features, such as seat size and number of wheels, gears, lights, and baskets. Your bike is make-believe, so you can include any features you want. It can be realistic or a wild bike of the future. It is your choice.

Next, write an ad for the bike. Your ad can be a basic picture with words, or it can be a composed paragraph. Remember, you are not trying to sell your bike to people your age. You are trying to sell it to grandparents! Think about what they need and like.

Snorkeling vs. Scuba Diving

DID YOU KNOW? Snorkeling is swimming on the surface of the water with a diving mask, a shaped tube called a *snorkel,* and usually swimming fins. The end of the snorkel has to stay out of the water so you can breathe.

Scuba diving is swimming completely underwater with a mask, breathing apparatus, and often a wetsuit. You have to be trained to scuba dive and use special equipment.

Activity: You are going on a summer vacation and you get to choose if you will go snorkeling or scuba diving. Choose one and explain why you prefer this activity. Think about the advantages and disadvantages, including cost, training, your comfort level in the water, and what you might see.

_____

_____

_____

_____

_____

_____

_____

_____

_____

_____

_____

_____

_____

_____

_____

_____

Underwater Adventure

IMAGINE THAT!

Imagine you are scuba diving. You choose where. Then think of an adventure you might have while scuba diving there.

Activity: Write two paragraphs in which you describe what happens. Will you find buried treasure or see sharks? Will you be attacked by a giant squid or hold on to the fin of a dolphin and take a ride? It is your choice.

_____

_____

_____

_____

_____

_____

_____

_____

_____

_____

_____

_____

_____

_____

_____

_____

_____

Manners

DID YOU KNOW?

What is polite and mannerly in one place may not be considered courteous in another place. For example, in Thailand, it is rude to pat a child on the head. It is also rude to leave your shoes on when entering someone's house. Instead, one should leave one's shoes neatly lined up at the door. Even when barefoot, one must be careful with one's feet. One should never point their feet at anyone or use their feet to move anything or touch anyone.

Activity: What is polite and mannerly where you live? Make a list of ten polite or mannerly things one can do. Think of words, phrases, and actions.

1. _____

2. _____

3. _____

4. _____

5. _____

6. _____

7. _____

8. _____

9. _____

10. _____

The Rude Child

Voice

Activity: Describe a scene in which a child is told over and over that he or she is rude because he or she is constantly interrupting. Have the child be told to wait until the adults are finished talking and say things like, "Excuse me," or "I'm sorry to interrupt." Finally, at the end of the story, have the child say, "Excuse me, I'm sorry to interrupt, but . . ."

You choose what the child tried to tell the adult. It can be humorous or some kind of disaster. For example, perhaps a broken pipe has caused a flood and the house is floating away, or an escaped tiger is asleep in the house. Use your imagination!

Fourth of July

Activity: Independence Day in the United States is on July 4. Describe the 4th of July (or your country's Independence Day). First, write a few sentences about your country's independence. When is it celebrated, and how did it come about?

Then, in a second paragraph, tell what you and your family do on Independence Day. Do you eat special foods? Do you go to school? Does your family do something together? Tell what your favorite part of the day is.

_____

_____

_____

_____

_____

_____

_____

_____

_____

_____

_____

_____

_____

_____

_____

_____

Independence Day

Activity: Write one or two paragraphs about your country's Independence Day, but do not write as yourself. Write as a child the same age as you but on your country's first Independence Day celebration—over 350 years ago! Tell about what you do, eat, and see during the day. Before you write, think about what types of things people might have eaten or drunk to celebrate. What kind of games or entertainment could there have been? For example, there could not be a car race, but there might be a horse race or a spelling bee.

Fortunately, Unfortunately

Voice

THINK ABOUT IT! You see a glass of water that has water up to the halfway mark. Is it half full or half empty? *Optimists* look on the bright side and see things in a positive perspective. An optimist says it is half full. *Pessimists* expect the worst and see things in a negative perspective. A pessimist says it is half empty.

Activity: Use complete sentences to describe how an optimist and a pessimist might see the same event. Start your sentences with the words *fortunately* or *unfortunately*. Your answers can be realistic or silly.

> **Example (for hurricane):**
>
> **Optimist:** *Fortunately, a hurricane is a wonderful time to study strong winds and see if your new rain boots have a hole in the sole.*
>
> **Pessimist:** *Unfortunately, a hurricane is a fierce wind that destroys homes and other buildings and breaks trees in half.*

Anaconda snake loose in the classroom

Optimist: _____

_____

Pessimist: _____

_____

The lights go out

Optimist: _____

_____

Pessimist: _____

_____

Math test today

Optimist: _____

_____

Pessimist: _____

_____

You are told a relative is coming to visit

Optimist: _____

_____

Pessimist: _____

_____

Organization

Long, Longer, Longest

Organization

THINK ABOUT IT! When writers compare the size, length, or weight of a group of similar objects, they organize their writing in a particular order. They usually talk about the objects in order from smallest to largest or largest to smallest. This will make the writing easier to follow.

Activity: Using the information about snakes below, write about snake sizes. You can go from shortest to longest or from longest to shortest. Just keep the order straight! Start your paragraph with a topic sentence in which you tell the reader what you are going to do. Add one or two details about each snake, but share the details immediately before or after you talk about size. This will keep your reader from getting confused.

Barbados Threadsnake: 4 in.; can coil up on a quarter; blind

Eastern Diamondback Rattlesnake: 8 ft.; has live young; can strike in the dark because it sees a "heat" image of its prey

King Cobra: 18.5 ft.; smells with tongue; kills with venom; can raise body, spread hood, and hiss to scare things away

Reticulated Python: 33 ft.; constrictor (suffocates prey); lays eggs; seen swimming in the ocean

_____

_____

_____

_____

_____

_____

_____

_____

_____

_____

_____

Pass the Chicken

Activity: Did you know snakes can be eaten? In fact, they can be a valuable food source. Write a story in which someone comes to dinner. The main course is rattlesnake in gravy. (Many people think rattlesnake has the same taste and texture as chicken.)

The guest does not know what he or she is eating and tells everyone during dinner that snakes are horrible. Have the guest ask for more and more "chicken." Will you tell the guest what he or she is eating, or will you just serve him or her more food? If you do tell, what does the guest do?

The Seven Continents

Activity: Show off what you know about the seven continents. Write at least two paragraphs. Your topic sentence should tell the reader that you will be discussing the continents, from largest to smallest or smallest to largest. Write two or three sentences about each continent.

List at least one animal and country for each continent. Then, select a fact to add. For example, name a language spoken there, or a mountain, desert, lake, or river found on the continent.

Example: *Antarctica is the fifth-largest continent. There aren't any polar bears, but there are a lot of seals. Antarctica is not divided into countries. There is a volcano on it.*

Plan ahead. Outline your paragraphs below and check off each box as you finish writing about it. Write your final paragraphs on another sheet of paper.

	Asia	Africa	N. America	S. America	Antarctica	Europe	Australia
Size							
Animal							
Country							
Fact							

_____

_____

_____

_____

_____

_____

_____

_____

_____

Polar Bear Cheating

Activity: Write a dialogue between you and your friend, grandmother, or other relative. Follow this basic plotline in your dialogue:

- Your grandmother tells you that someone has asked her to donate a lot of money. The funds would help save polar bears in Antarctica.

- You tell her to not give any money.

- Your grandmother thinks you don't want to save polar bears.

- You tell her it is a trick—polar bears don't live in Antarctica!

When you write, use words and expressions that make it sound like a real conversation.

_____

_____

_____

_____

_____

_____

_____

_____

_____

_____

_____

_____

_____

_____

_____

_____

Polar Bears

THINK ABOUT IT! The words that writers choose for their opening sentences help readers decide if they want to continue reading. Which topic sentence below will grab the reader's attention?

Polar bears can smell. OR **Polar bears are called "noses with legs."**

Activity: Copy the topic sentence above that you chose, and then finish the paragraph. Use the facts in the fact box below to help you. Write a second paragraph about polar bear feet. Can you think of a fun sentence that will grab the reader's attention?

Polar Bear Nose Facts	Polar Bear Feet Facts
• longer nose than other bears (powerful sense of smell) • can smell a seal on ice 20 miles away • can sniff out a seal's den covered with three or four feet of snow • will cover its dark nose with paw to keep from being seen	• only front paws used for swimming • front paws are webbed like a duck's • Paw is about 12 inches wide, 18 inches long • rear feet used to steer, like rudders • all paws have rough pads and stiff, thick fur which prevents slipping on ice

_____

_____

_____

_____

_____

_____

_____

_____

_____

The Race

DID YOU KNOW? Did you know Michael Phelps has size 14 feet? His big feet are like paddles, which have helped him win Olympic medals!

Activity: Write a story in which someone doesn't like his or her big feet. Tell how the person feels. Do people tease him or her? Then think of a time when someone has to swim. It may be in a race or to save someone who is drowning. You choose. Who is the fastest swimmer? The person with the big feet!

_____

_____

_____

_____

_____

_____

_____

_____

_____

_____

_____

_____

_____

_____

_____

_____

_____

The Ice-Cream Cone

Activity: In stories, it is important to write what happens in the right order. If you don't, the story doesn't make sense. Order the lines below so that they make sense.

_____ Then everyone at the fair wanted ice cream in a cone.

____2____ Arnold Fornachou ran out of paper dishes for ice cream at the fair.

____6____ Hamwi showed people all over the country the new way to eat ice cream after the fair.

____4____ Fornachou sold his ice cream in Hamwi's cones.

_____ Hamwi was given a patent for a cone-making machine in 1920.

_____ The 1904 World's Fair was in St. Louis, Missouri.

_____ Ernest Hamwi rolled up some of his waffle-like pastry into cones.

Activity: Now write a complete story using the events above. Include a title for your story that catches the reader's attention. Make sure the actions in your story are in the right order. Add or change words to the lines above so that the story flows smoothly.

_____

_____

_____

_____

_____

_____

_____

_____

_____

Ice-Cream Battle

THINK ABOUT IT!

A story almost always has an ending or a conclusion. Some stories have conclusions that make one think.

Activity: Write a story with an ending that makes the reader think. In your story, have two characters fighting over ice cream. They are fighting over how to divide it evenly. Who should serve, and who should pick what bowl first? Then have the characters discover that, while they were fighting, all the ice cream melted or someone else ate it. For your final line, tell what lesson the characters learned.

Make sure that when you write, you describe your events in order. You do not want the characters in the story to know the ice cream has melted until the end. If you let the reader know too soon, the ending won't be a surprise.

_____

_____

_____

_____

_____

_____

_____

_____

_____

_____

_____

_____

New Holiday

DID YOU KNOW? A federal holiday is a government holiday. Some federal holidays are New Year's Day, Independence Day, George Washington's birthday, Martin Luther King Jr.'s birthday, and Christmas Day.

How does a day become a holiday? Congress must approve it. The president must give his or her signature. State and local holidays don't need the president's signature. They just need the approval of the state and local government.

Activity: Imagine that you are going to ask for a day to become a new holiday. First, think of a reason for a new holiday. Decide if your new holiday will be a federal, state, or local holiday. It could be to celebrate someone, to remember an event, or to volunteer. Then write a paragraph in which you describe the new holiday. Tell why or for whom it is a holiday. Tell what day it should be celebrated on and why. Describe the types of activities people might do on this day.

_____

_____

_____

_____

_____

_____

_____

_____

_____

_____

_____

_____

_____

Forgotten Birthday

Activity: Make up a story in which it is someone's birthday. This person gets up, all excited about the day. All through the day he or she keeps hoping someone will remember his or her birthday. No one seems to care or know, which makes the person become sadder and sadder. Finally, there is a surprise party at the end of the story.

Plan ahead when you write. Make the reader feel sad for the person. Don't let the reader know what will happen until the very end. Think about where and how to surprise the person. Once you have finished writing your story, add an appropriate title.

Brazil Letter

Activity: You are writing a letter to a friend. The friend thinks the country of Brazil and your country are alike. In your letter, tell your friend how the two countries differ.

Your letter should have two paragraphs. The first paragraph should describe Brazil. The second paragraph should describe your country. When you write, you need to stay organized. Discuss things in the same order. For example, if the first thing you wrote about was on what continent and in what hemisphere Brazil is located, then the first thing you should write about your country is where it is located, too. Plan ahead by filling in the information for your country in the chart. If necessary, continue your letter on the back of this page.

Brazil	(your country)_____
• in South America • Southern Hemisphere • capital: Brasilia • main language: Portuguese • Amazon River, huge tropical rainforests • jaguars, toucans, monkeys • Independence Day: September 7, 1822	

Dear _____ ,

My country is called _____ , and there are many differences

between it and Brazil. _____

_____

_____

_____

_____

Letter from Brazil

Activity: Pretend you have gone to Brazil. Write a letter to a friend back home. Use the information in the fact boxes below to imagine an adventure you might have. Your letter should have two paragraphs. The first paragraph should describe jaguars. Your second paragraph should describe how you were stitched up by ants.

Jaguar Facts	Army Ant Facts
largest cats in Western Hemisphere	ants used for stitches
enjoy swimming	cut is pressed together, and ant seizes edges of wound in jaws; body then cut off, and head and jaws remain in wound as a stitch
may go fishing by waving tail over water to attract fish	

School Life

THINK ABOUT IT! Diaries written long ago help us to learn how life used to be. For example, some people from colonial times wrote in their diaries about their schools. They wrote about things such as boys and girls sitting separately, about sitting on hard benches, and about children having to bring sticks of wood to class. What happened to the children who forgot their wood? They had to sit farthest from the warm stove!

Activity: Write two diary entries about your school. Imagine that one day someone will learn about your school from these entries. For that reason, stay organized. Describe your school in general in the first entry. Talk about things such as students, grades, location, size, food, calendar, and playgrounds. In your second entry, make it personal. Describe your class specifically, what you are learning, and what your favorite subject is. Talk about a recent project or a book you read.

This journal belongs to _____

Date: _____   _____

_____

_____

_____

_____

_____

Date: _____   _____

_____

_____

_____

_____

School on Mars

IMAGINE THAT!

Imagine that it is the future. You are a student at school, but you are not on Earth. You are on Mars!

Activity: Write two diary entries about your school day there. In your first entry, describe your school in general. Talk about things such as students, grades, location, size, food, calendar, and playgrounds. In your second entry, make it personal. Describe your class specifically, what you are learning, and what your favorite subject is. Talk about a recent project or a book you read.

Before you write, think about Mars. Will you be able to go outside? Will books and writing be a thing of the past? Will the teacher be on Earth and speak to you through a computer? Use your imagination!

This journal belongs to _____

Date: _____

_____

_____

_____

_____

_____

Date: _____

_____

_____

_____

_____

_____

Jump from Space

Activity: News reports tell *who, what, where, when, why,* and sometimes *how* things happened. Use the facts below to write a news report using words that make it exciting to read. Also, try to make your sentences flow together. When you are done, add a headline that catches the reader's attention.

Who: Capt. Joseph Kittinger   **What:** record high parachute jump

Where: 102,800 feet above Earth from open balloon basket *Excelsior III*

When: August 16, 1960   **Why:** testing if people could survive high altitudes

How: jumped into black space, below zero temperature (minus 94°F), wearing special suit

Trip Details: fell at 614 miles per hour (almost the speed of sound!), hand swelled to two times normal size because of mistake in suit

---

_____

By: _____

Body Voyage

IMAGINE THAT!

Imagine that it is the future. You (or another character) are the first to be shrunk to a tiny size. Then you (or the character) travel through a sick person's body and fix what is wrong. You choose who the patient is, what is wrong, what organs you visit, what needs to be done to save the patient, and how you enter and leave the body.

Activity: Write a newspaper article about the trip. Use what you know about the body and how it works to make your story sound real. Include many adventures. Plan ahead by filling in the chart below before you write your story.

Who: _____

What: _____

Where: _____

When: _____

Why: _____

How: _____

Trip Details: _____

_____

By: _____

_____   _____

_____   _____

_____   _____

_____   _____

_____   _____

Dressed for School

Organization

DID YOU KNOW? Transition words are words such as the following: *for example, when, soon, after, first, before, finally, next, now, then, immediately, suddenly.* Using these words will help your sentences flow together.

Activity: Write a paragraph in which you are the narrator, telling how you get dressed in the morning. You will use the word *I* since you are the narrator. Include many details and think about order. For example, do you tie your shoes before you put them on? Do you put your coat on before your shirt? Also, tell where you get your clothes from. For example, do you get your pants from the refrigerator or a dresser?

Plan ahead. What clothing items will you put on, in what order, and where will you get them from?

	Item	Where Item Is Kept
1.		
2.		
3.		
4.		
5.		

_____

_____

_____

_____

_____

_____

_____

_____

_____

Lost at Sea

THINK ABOUT IT! Using transition words will help your writing flow. Transition words include the following: *for example, when, soon, after, first, before, finally, next, now, then, immediately, suddenly.*

Activity: Write a story in which two people are lost and scared. The people see all kinds of animals that live underwater, such as sharks, barracuda, huge clams, meat-eating piranha, and more! Make it seem as if the people are under the water. At the end, reveal that the people are not under the water. They are at an aquarium! They just got separated from their class or friends.

When you write, try to use as many transition words as you can. Transition words will help your story flow smoothly as you take your characters from one underwater animal to the next.

_____

_____

_____

_____

_____

_____

_____

_____

_____

_____

THINK ABOUT IT!

Someone is learning English. He or she asks you, "I got a message. It says I have to do something ASAP. What does *ASAP* mean?"

Activity: Write a paragraph in which you explain what *ASAP* means. First say what it is, and then explain what each letter means. Provide at least two examples of when it might be used. One example should be general. For example, a faucet breaks, and water is pouring out everywhere. You call the plumber and say, "I need you ASAP!" The second example should be personal. What was a time in your life when you did or needed something ASAP?

ASAP is an acronym.*

A = as   S = soon   A = as   P = possible

*An acronym is a word formed from the first letters of words in a name or phrase.

Taking L, MARTA, and BART

DID YOU KNOW?

Many cities have trains. The trains are known by their acronyms. For example, the train system in Atlanta, Georgia, is known as MARTA (Metropolitan Atlanta Rapid Transit Authority). In San Francisco, it is known as BART (Bay Area Rapid Transit). In Chicago, it is known as L.

Activity: Select L, MARTA, or BART. Then write a dialogue in which a new student comes to school and hears other students say things such as, "I'm going shopping, so I'll take MARTA." "I'm going to take BART to the baseball game." "Let's take L downtown."

The new student does not know the acronyms for the trains. The student thinks the acronyms are real people! Finally, have the new student say that he or she needs to meet L, Marta, or Bart because they seem to know everyone! Then explain to the newcomer what the L, MARTA, or BART really is.

_____

_____

_____

_____

_____

_____

_____

_____

_____

_____

_____

_____

_____

Biography

DID YOU KNOW?

A *biography* is the story of someone's life written by someone else. (If you write your own biography, it is called an *autobiography*.)

Activity: Think of a close relative or friend. Write a two-paragraph biography about him or her. Stay organized when you write! Don't jump from past to present back to past. Try to stay on a timeline.

Focus on the past in the first paragraph. Discuss birth, family, schooling, and growing up. In the second paragraph, focus on the present. Where is the person living now, with whom, and what is he or she doing? What are the person's likes and dislikes?

Is there a big event that changed this person's life? Should you describe that event in the first or second paragraph?

Autobiography

IMAGINE THAT!

Imagine that you are an animal. You can be a wild animal or a domestic animal. (A domestic animal is one that is tame or taken care of by people.)

Activity: Write a two-paragraph autobiography about your life as an animal. Remember to use the word *I* because you are the narrator.

First paragraph: Decide what kind of animal you are (wild or domestic). Talk about how you were born (from an egg? in a litter?). Discuss where you live, what you eat, and what you have to watch out for.

Second paragraph: Describe a big event. It may be something such as the day you caught your first meal, the day you learned to swim or fly, or the day you escaped from a predator. Include many details.

_____

_____

_____

_____

_____

_____

_____

_____

_____

_____

_____

Ericson's Voyage

Activity: Leif Ericson was an explorer. Write a paragraph first telling who Ericson was and what he is known for. Then describe his trip. Use transition words such as *first, second, next, after, before,* and *finally* to make your sentences read smoothly. For your final sentences, explain why or why not you think Leif Ericson Day should be a federal holiday.

Leif Ericson—Norse (Norwegian) Explorer

- celebrated for being first European to stand on North American soil
- born in Iceland in 970
- grew up in Greenland
- 1002 or 1003, sailed west with 35 crew members
- first landing believed to be in Labrador, Canada
- next landing believed to be in Newfoundland, Canada
- third landing could be northern Newfoundland or Cape Cod, United States
- In 1964, President Johnson, with support of Congress, said October 9 was "Leif Ericson Day."

_____

_____

_____

_____

_____

_____

_____

_____

_____

_____

_____

Thor is a mythical Norse god. Norse myths came from the countries of Sweden, Norway, Iceland, and Denmark. Thor was the god of thunder. He had red, flowing hair, eyes of lightning, and a chariot that was pulled by goats that he rode across the sky during thunderstorms. Lightning flashed when Thor threw his magic hammer, which always returned to him. Thor wore iron gloves and a belt that made him twice as strong. People liked Thor because he protected animals and people from evil.

Activity: Write a paragraph about an adventure Thor has. Thor can fight a dragon, a giant, or any other type of beast. He can save a sailor or anyone else. It is your story, so use your imagination! Plan ahead by listing some notes in each box before you start writing.

Setting	Characters	Action	Ending

_____

_____

_____

_____

_____

_____

_____

_____

_____

It's a Sale!

Look at the sale ad to the right. Why might no one go to this sale? Choose two reasons below.

1. The prices sound too high.

2. It doesn't say what items are for sale.

3. It doesn't say the time of the sale.

4. It doesn't say where the sale is.

Activity: Create an ad for a sale. You choose what is for sale. The ad can be for a real store, a sale you make up, or a school fundraiser. Use persuasive words and phrases that will make people want to come.

Stay organized by planning ahead. Complete the details in the chart, and then design the ad in the box below.

Huge sale today!

Top Bargains!

Something for Everyone!

Lowest Prices!

Sale runs for four hours only.

2:00 p.m. to 6:00 p.m.

What: _____

When: _____

Where: _____

Why: _____

How Long: _____

Conventions

Rowing Across the Ocean

Reminder: Capital letters are used . . .

- at the start of sentences. (**T**he monkey is eating.)
- in proper names or the word *I*. (**N**ew **Y**ork is where **I** live.)
- in titles of books, songs, movies, and articles (short words like *a* and *the* are not capitalized unless they are the first word). (**T**he **B**oy and the **W**olf)

Activity: Read the paragraph and add proofreading marks where needed. You will need to add the following:

- 11 marks for uppercase letters   Example: arizona
- 6 marks for lowercase letters   Example: Two

> huge whales dove under the tiny Boat and surfaced right next to the *pilot*. The *pilot*, only 24-feet long, rocked dangerously. Would the Whales crush the boat? the french woman, maud fontenoy, was terrified. Maud was trying to row across the North atlantic Ocean. She was going West to East. no woman had ever done this. maud rowed for 117 Days. despite whales, sharks, and Icebergs, Maud did it!

Activity: Now show what you know! Write a short paragraph with at least five sentences. In your paragraph, tell what you would do if you had a boat. What kind of boat would you like, and where would you go? Would you fish, sail, row, motor, or waterski? Would you rather go on long or short trips?

Include five uppercase and five lowercase letter errors in your writing. Write the incorrect words correctly on the back of this page. Show your test paragraph to your classmates. Could they spot the errors?

_____

_____

_____

_____

_____

_____

Cries for Help

Reminder: Capital letters are used . . .

- at the start of sentences. (**P**lease take one.)
- in proper names or the word *I*. (**I** live in **S**alem, **O**regon.)
- titles of books, songs, movies, and articles (short words like *a* and *the* are not capitalized unless they are the first word). (**T**he **D**ay the **T**rains **S**topped)

Activity: Read the paragraph and add proofreading marks where needed. You will need to add the following:

- 11 marks for uppercase letters   Example: <u>m</u>aine
- 7 marks for lowercase letters   Example: ⊤welve

> Dan lived in sheepville, wyoming. Dan's Job was to take the Sheep out to graze. On monday, august 3, Dan cried, "i see a Wolf!" Mr. Trace, the Rancher, came running, but there was no Wolf. Dan yelled, "i see a wolf" on Tuesday, wednesday, and Thursday. every day the rancher came running. then on friday, Dan saw a Real wolf and cried for Help. What do you think mr. Trace did?

Activity: Now show what you know! Write a similar story as the one above, but place it in the city. Choose your characters. Will they yell for help about a cat, dog, mouse, rat, spider, snake, fire, or even an ice-cream truck? It is up to you what happens!

Include five uppercase and five lowercase letter errors in your writing. Write the incorrect words correctly on the back of this page. Show your test paragraph to your classmates. Could they spot the errors?

_____

_____

_____

_____

_____

_____

_____

Activity: Read the paragraph and add proofreading marks where needed. You will need to add the following:

- 5 periods (.)
- 2 question marks (?)
- 1 exclamation mark (!)

A skyscraper is a tall building on land Did you know that the term *skyscraper* came from a sailing term On old sailing ships, the skyscraper was a small, triangular sail that was set above the skysail

In the late 19th century, buildings were framed with steel   This allowed them to be built much higher People were astounded at the first 10-story buildings What did they call these tall buildings They called them *skyscrapers*! What would those people think of skyscrapers today? One skyscraper in Dubai has 163 floors and is 2,717 feet high

Activity: Now show what you know! Write a paragraph in which you describe the highest building you have ever seen. Then give two advantages and two disadvantages to living in a skyscraper.

Include five ending punctuation errors in your paragraph. Show the correct editing marks, or have another student find and mark the mistakes.

_____

_____

_____

_____

_____

_____

_____

_____

_____

Races

Activity: Read the paragraph and add proofreading marks where needed. You will need to add the following:

- 2 periods (.)
- 3 question marks (**?**)
- 1 exclamation mark (**!**)

> Where do most running races take place They take place on trails, streets, or tracks There are some races that do not happen on any of these places Where could the races take place Amazingly, they take place in skyscrapers Athletes travel around the world to enter these races. How fast do you think you can run up 163 flights of stairs

Activity: Now show what you know! Write a short story about a character who is always getting in trouble for running up and down stairs. Then the character becomes the youngest world champion of skyscraper running!

When you are done, review what you have written. Check for capital letters and ending punctuation marks.

_____

_____

_____

_____

_____

_____

_____

_____

_____

_____

The Note

THINK ABOUT IT! A real estate agent helps people buy and sell houses. What if a real estate agent got this note: "You need to go buy the house. Sheila will go buy two." How many houses will be bought? _____

What if the note was meant to say this: "You need to go by the house. Sheila will go by, too." Now how many houses will be bought? _____

Activity: Simple spelling errors like this can change the meaning of something very important. Write a few lines in which you explain the importance of spelling. Then explain what the words *buy*, *by*, *too*, *two*, and *to* mean. Use them correctly in example sentences.

Pie with the Principal

Activity: Write a dialogue between two people. One character can't remember the difference between *peace* and *piece* and *principal* and *principle*. Have the other character explain what these words mean and give hints on how to remember them.

> **peace**—calmness; no fighting   **principle**—a rule or belief
>
> **piece**—a part   **principal**—head of a school
>
> **Hints:** You can eat a <u>pie</u>ce of <u>pie</u>. A princip<u>al</u> is your <u>pal</u>.

_____

_____

_____

_____

_____

_____

_____

_____

_____

_____

_____

_____

_____

_____

_____

_____

Neighbors

THINK ABOUT IT!

When you write, you need to check your spelling. The reader takes your writing more seriously if the words are spelled correctly. The reader will also know exactly what you mean. There is a list of the 100 most commonly misspelled words. What words are on the list? One word is *neighbor*. People forget to put the *e* before the *i*.

Activity: Read the paragraph in the box below. Cross out the three misspelled words by putting an **X** on them.

> How many country nieghbors do you have? The countries with the most neighbors are China and Russia. They both have 14 neighbors! Brazil has ten nieghbors. Countries like Australia and Japan do not have any nieghbors.

Activity: Write a paragraph in which you describe a neighbor. The neighbor can be a family member, an individual, a class, or a country. Explain in the first sentence what type of neighbor you are writing about. Then add many details so there is no mistaking what neighbor it is!

When you write, use the word *neighbor* at least two times. Make sure you put the *e* before the *i*!

_____

_____

_____

_____

_____

_____

_____

_____

_____

_____

Wrong Neighbor!

Activity: Write a story in which you or another character goes to England. You turn in a school paper in which you discuss the United Kingdom's neighbors. When your paper comes back, it is marked wrong. You tell the teacher your neighbor facts are correct. The teacher says you've misspelled *neighbor*. In the United Kingdom, *neighbor* is spelled *neighbour*! Use the information in the box when writing your story.

United Kingdom Facts

The United Kingdom is made up of the following countries: England, Scotland, Wales, and Northern Ireland.

The only land neighbor of the United Kingdom is Ireland.

In England, it is *colour*, not *color*; *flavour*, not *flavor*; *honour*, not *honor*.

_____

_____

_____

_____

_____

_____

_____

_____

_____

_____

_____

_____

Their, There, They're

THINK ABOUT IT!

The words *they're*, *their*, and *there* are often misspelled and/or used incorrectly. They are on the list of the 100 most commonly misspelled words. The three words sound the same, but they do not mean the same thing. You want people to know what you mean when you write. You want people to take your writing seriously, so you want to use the right word.

They're means "they are." (Example: They're tired, so they slept late.)

Their is possessive, meaning something belongs to them. (Example: Their dog is big.)

There is for everything else, usually to represent a place. (Example: We went there after school.)

Activity: Cross out the misspelled words in the sentences below. Then write the correct spelling on the line.

Their from Indiana.   _____

There capital is Indianapolis.   _____

The Indianapolis 500 Race takes place they're.   _____

They grow corn their.   _____

Activity: Write about people from three different states. Use *there*, *they're*, and *their* in each description.

1. _____

   _____

   _____

2. _____

   _____

   _____

3. _____

   _____

   _____

Review your spelling. If you can say "they are" the word should be spelled *they're*. If it is possessive, it should be spelled *their*. Everything else is *there*.

Field Trip Money

A note was sent to all the parents in your school. The note said this:

> *Dear Parents,*
>
> *The students in our school are doing well, but there in great need. Every year their is a field trip for which we need money. Please send money for they're field trip to there treasurer.*
>
> *Thank you,*
>
> *Principle Gabe Lincoln*

All the fifth-grade students told their parents, "The note is not real."

Activity: Explain why the students knew the note was not real. Tell how they checked to see what form of *there* should be used. Then go back and correct the misspelled words.

Extra: There are five misspelled words in the note. Four of them are *they're, their,* or *there* misspellings. Can you spot the fifth misspelled word?

_____

_____

_____

_____

_____

_____

_____

_____

_____

Hermit Crabs

You can make two short sentences into one long one by doing two things.

   1. Place a comma (,) after the first sentence.

   2. Then add the words *and, or,* or *but* between the sentences.

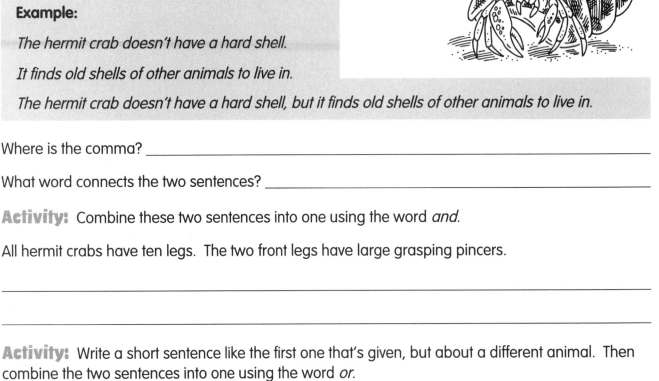

Example:

The hermit crab doesn't have a hard shell.

It finds old shells of other animals to live in.

The hermit crab doesn't have a hard shell, but it finds old shells of other animals to live in.

Where is the comma? _____

What word connects the two sentences? _____

Activity: Combine these two sentences into one using the word *and.*

All hermit crabs have ten legs. The two front legs have large grasping pincers.

_____

_____

Activity: Write a short sentence like the first one that's given, but about a different animal. Then combine the two sentences into one using the word *or.*

short: I would like to see a hermit crab.

short: _____

long: _____

_____

Activity: Now write two short sentences of your own. Then combine them into one long sentence using the word *and, or,* or *but.*

short: _____

short: _____

long: _____

_____

When you are done, go back and read your long sentences. Did you remember to add commas?

Buying a House

Activity: Write a short story with this plotline: a character (a student your age) says he is going to buy a house. No one believes him; after all, how could a young person buy a house? The character gets teased. What type of house is the character buying? It is a new, bigger shell for his pet hermit crab!

When you write, make at least two long sentences by combining two short sentences using the word *and*, *or*, or *but*.

Now go back and review what you have written. Check your spelling. Check your punctuation. Did you remember to put the comma before *and*, *or*, or *but* when you joined two complete sentences together?

How do we quote people when we write about them? What punctuation marks tell us that these are words that the person said or is saying? We put their words in quotation marks (" "). We put commas (,) to separate their words from the rest of the sentence.

Activity: Look at the example. Circle the commas and quotation marks.

> Thomas Alva Edison was a famous inventor. He held patents for 1,093 inventions! One of his most famous inventions is the light bulb. What did Edison say about all his inventions? He said, "I never did anything by accident, nor did any of my inventions come by accident; they came by hard work."

Did the comma go before or after the quotation mark? _____

Did the period go before or after the quotation mark? _____

Activity: Fix the sentence below by adding the missing period, comma, and quotation marks.

> Edison said Genius is one percent inspiration and 99 percent perspiration

Activity: Now it is your turn to write! Write a paragraph explaining what you think Edison meant when he said, "I have not failed. I've just found 10,000 ways that won't work." Use the following as a guide:

First lines: Say who Edison was and the quote you are writing about.

Middle: Tell what you think he means. (If you want to include any or both of the first two quotes, you can.)

End: Tell what you personally can learn from this.

_____

_____

_____

_____

_____

Activity: Write a conversation between different kinds of animals. Have the animals debate as to what skin or fur color is the best. Have the animals explain why they think so.

When you write, change the start of your sentences by using words such as *barked, roared, neighed, mooed, growled, hissed,* or *laughed* before your quotes.

Example: *Hyena laughed meanly, "Only a fool would want to be bright white here on the savannah. Light brown is the best color, and my dark-brown spots help me blend in and make me even more beautiful!"*

When you are done, review what you have written. Check your commas and quotation marks!

_____

_____

_____

_____

_____

_____

_____

_____

_____

_____

_____

_____

_____

Activity: Write "one deer" or "more than one" deer on the lines.

The female deer is the one without antlers. _____

The female deer are the ones without antlers. _____

What words in the sentences helped you know if there were one or more deer?

is and *are*, *one* and *ones*

When you write, you need to make sure you have subject-verb agreement. You have to use the correct form of the verb with the subject.

Activity: Rewrite the paragraph below, changing all the underlined single nouns to plural nouns. Also change the verb form to match. You will have to change other words, too, for your sentences to make sense.

A <u>mouse</u> does not have antlers. A <u>wolf</u> does not have antlers. A male <u>moose</u> has antlers, but a <u>female</u> does not. Only a female <u>reindeer</u> or <u>caribou</u> has antlers. An <u>antler</u> is not a horn. An <u>antler</u> is made up of solid bone, and <u>it</u> is shed yearly. A <u>horn</u> is different. Only the inside of a <u>horn</u> is bone, and <u>it</u> does not fall off.

Plurals

mouse—mice

wolf—wolves

moose—moose

reindeer—reindeer

caribou—caribou

_____

_____

_____

_____

_____

_____

_____

_____

Now go back and review what you have written. Did you change all the things you needed to?

The Alien

IMAGINE THAT!

Imagine that you hear a knock on the door. You open it, and there is an alien!

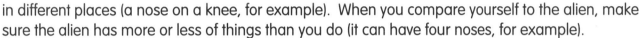

Activity: Write two paragraphs about your experience. In the first paragraph, you set the scene by telling about opening the door, and how you feel when you see the alien.

In the second paragraph, describe and compare yourself to the alien. The alien can be any shape or color that you want. It can have things in different places (a nose on a knee, for example). When you compare yourself to the alien, make sure the alien has more or less of things than you do (it can have four noses, for example).

When you are done, review what you have written. Make sure you spelled the singular and plural form of nouns correctly (tooth and teeth) and you have subject-verb agreement. (My *nose* is on my face. His *noses are* on his knees.)

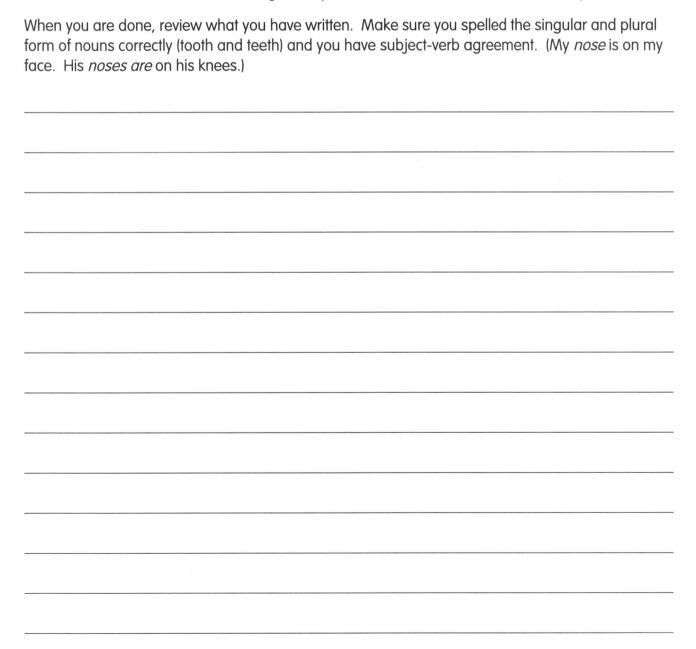

Who Said "Stop"?

Activity: Underline the verb in each sentence. The verb is the action word. It tells what the person did.

Betty plodded through the park.   **Carlos raced through the park.**

Frieda tore through the park.   **Ethan marched through the park.**

Activity: Use the verbs to help you choose what each person from above did. Each name is only used once. Write down the name and then explain why you think the person could be doing this.

was trying to get away from an escaped bear: _____

was seeing who could go fastest: _____

was really tired: _____

was in a parade: _____

Using the verbs helps you picture how (in order) Frieda, Carlos, Betty, and Ethan match the activities above.

Activity: Now it is your turn! Think of two bears. One bear is wild, and the other is a teddy bear. Write about how the wild bear makes you feel in one box. Write about how the teddy bear makes you feel in the second box. Write three or four sentences in each box. Use verbs that help the reader understand how you are feeling. Then share your sentences with other students. Could they tell which box was about what bear?

```
Box 1
_____

_____

_____

_____
```

```
Box 2
_____

_____

_____

_____
```

Bear on the Bed

Activity: Write a short story with this plotline: a small child tells adults that there is a bear on his bed (or in his room). All the adults think the bear is a teddy bear. The truth comes out in a surprise ending. The bear is real, and it has escaped from the circus or zoo!

Your story should have at least two paragraphs. Use verbs that help readers form a picture in their minds. Perhaps you can have the adults laugh, smile, and tease at first. At the end, they can gasp, tremble, and shake. When you are done, review what you have written. Check your spelling, punctuation, and grammar.

_____

_____

_____

_____

_____

_____

_____

_____

_____

_____

_____

_____

The Same Boat

DID YOU KNOW? What is an idiom? An idiom is a natural way of speaking. Idioms may be hard to understand if you are a non-native English speaker or are learning a new language. "All in the same boat" is an idiom. If taken literally, it is taken exactly as written. It means that everyone is actually in the same boat. As an idiom, it usually means that people aren't in a boat at all. Instead, the people are in the same situation and are all facing the same problem.

Activity: In which sentence is the phrase "all in the same boat" used as an idiom?

1. We were all in the same boat when we went fishing.

2. We were all in the same boat when it came to finding clothes for the dance.

Activity: Now write two paragraphs about the idiom "bite your tongue" following this guide.

Paragraph One: Explain what an idiom is. Tell what *bite your tongue* means literally. Tell what *bite your tongue* means as an idiom (to keep quiet). Tell why an English language learner might need to know this.

Paragraph Two: Tell about a time when you had to bite or should have bitten your tongue.

_____

_____

_____

_____

_____

_____

_____

_____

_____

_____

_____

Medicine Taste

Conventions

THINK ABOUT IT!

An idiom is a phrase that means something other than what the words seem to mean. The following are some examples of idioms:

- a taste of your own medicine (someone does something bad to you that you had done to them to teach you a lesson)
- against the clock (do something in a great hurry with little time to spare)
- chip on your shoulder (to feel resentful about something; have a bad attitude)

Activity: Choose an idiom from above or another one you know. Tell a story about a new student who is learning English. Describe or write a small scene during which an idiom is used. The new student gets very confused because he or she takes the idiom literally. He or she does not know what it really means. You can write your scene in paragraph or dialogue form.

Proofreading Marks

Proofreading is when you read over what you have written to check for mistakes. How do proofreaders show what is incorrect? They use certain marks, such as the following:

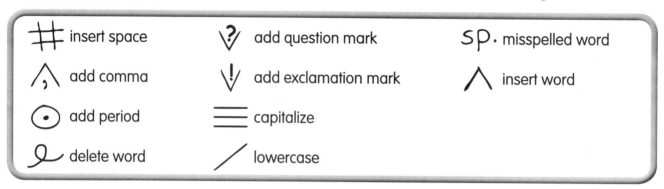

# insert space	?/ add question mark	SP. misspelled word
∧, add comma	!/ add exclamation mark	∧ insert word
⊙ add period	≡ capitalize	
ℓ delete word	/ lowercase	

Activity: Proofread the passage below. Add the proofreading marks as needed to correct the mistakes. You will need the following:

- 2 insert words
- 3 add periods
- 2 capitalize letters

- 1 delete word
- 1 add question mark
- 2 lowercase letters

- 1 add comma
- 1 insert space
- 3 misspelled words

we have two remember to take a life jacket with us but a walrus never has to remember. why don't walruses have to remember they're life jackets A walrus's life jacket   built in Walruses have two pouches or air Sacs in their necks The sacs can hold 13 gallons ofair. When the sacs are Filled, walruses can float vertically They can float straight straight up with there heads out the water.

Activity: Now show what you know! Write some sentences about you and life jackets. Share times when you have used or should use a life jacket. Tell what kind of life jackets you are familiar with. Are there times you don't use a life jacket? Where and why? Include some mistakes in your sentences. Then mark the mistakes with the correct proofreading marks.

_____

_____

_____

_____

_____

What Did I Eat?

Activity: Read the following sentences and add four proofreading marks where needed to correct the mistakes.

> walruses do not see well, but their whiskers Help them find food. The walrus whiskers is not hair. They are tactile organs that help them find food by touch

Activity: Now write a story in which a character decides to be like a walrus. The character puts on a blindfold and says he or she will find food by touch. Describe a scene in which the character finds some food and eats it. When it is in his or her mouth, the character gets a surprise! What was put in his or her mouth is not what he or she expected!

Think ahead—what does the character think he or she has? What does it end up being?

When you are done with your story, review what you have written. Add proofreading marks when necessary.

_____

_____

_____

_____

_____

_____

_____

_____

_____

_____

School Uniforms

DID YOU KNOW?

All schools have dress codes. Some dress codes are strict, and students must wear uniforms. Some dress codes are not as strict. There may only be rules about shoes or words and pictures on clothes.

Activity: Should your school have a different dress code, or should it remain exactly the same? Write a letter to your school board. Include two paragraphs in your letter. Introduce yourself in the first paragraph. Tell what grade you are in, who your teacher is, and how long you have attended the school. Then tell them that it has been brought to your attention that there might be dress code changes. Tell them you want to address this issue.

State what you want in the second paragraph. Give reasons why this is for the best. Give a personal example to strengthen your argument.

Dear School Board Members:

_____

_____

_____

_____

_____

_____

_____

_____

_____

_____

Now proofread your letter. Check your grammar, punctuation, and spelling. This way, people will focus on your message instead of your mistakes.

Invisible Cloak

Activity: Imagine that you invented a cloak (a loose jacket). The cloak made you invisible! Write a two-paragraph letter to a friend. Because the letter is to a friend, you do not have to be formal.

Paragraph One: greetings; tell why you are writing (give cloak details)

Paragraph Two: an adventure you had with the cloak

Dear _____ ,

_____

_____

_____

_____

_____

_____

_____

_____

_____

_____

_____

_____

_____

_____

_____

IMAGINE THAT!

Titles are important. They need to fit the subject, and they must be correctly punctuated. Imagine that you or someone else wrote a book about your life. The chapter number matches your age.

Activity: Write a title for each chapter. Your chapter titles can be humorous or serious. Think about what you might be doing when you are older and write titles for later years. Imagine, too, if you end up living until age 125 and what it would be like to be the world's oldest person!

When you write titles, remember these rules:

- Always capitalize the first and last words of a title, even if they are short.
- Capitalize all important words (verbs, nouns, pronouns, most adverbs, and adjectives).
- Do not capitalize most short words (*and*, *for*, *a*, *the*).

Practice by correcting the mistakes in these titles. Then write the titles for the chapters in a book about your life.

the year i Won the Game   (3 mistakes) _____

Astronaut At last!   (2 mistakes) _____

Chapter 1: _____

Chapter 2: _____

Chapter 3: _____

Chapter 4: _____

Chapter 5: _____

Chapter 6: _____

Chapter 7: _____

Chapter 8: _____

Chapter 9: _____

Chapter 10: _____

Chapter 20: _____

Chapter 50: _____

Chapter 100: _____

Chapter 125: _____

Writing Prompts

Prompt 1

You can be a bird for a day. What kind of bird would you like to be and why? Think about where you would live, what you would eat, predators, and general habits. In a second paragraph, tell about an adventure you might have.

Prompt 2

I gasped when I looked at the reflection in the mirror. It wasn't my face! Yet when I smiled, the face smiled. Who was I? What had happened to me?

Prompt 3

Bananas are the best-selling fruit in the United States. Do you buy more bananas than other fruits? Discuss your fruit-eating habits. What fruit do you eat most, and what fruit do you like the best and least? Do you like your fruit raw, cooked, or mixed with other foods?

Prompt 4

"You've won!" screamed Terry's brother in excitement! . . .

Prompt 5

Describe four things that you like about yourself or that you can do well. Give some details. Why did you choose these things, and/or how did you learn to do them?

Prompt 6

The hair on the back of Paula's neck seemed to stand up when . . .

Prompt 7

Would you rather be captain of a submarine or a boat? Explain why. Tell where you might take your crew if you could take them anywhere you wanted.

Prompt 8

"Get out of the way!" cried Sam, "It's coming right for us!" . . .

Prompt 9

Benjamin Franklin once wrote, "Beware of little expenses. A small leak will sink a great ship." What do you think he meant? Was he only talking about sailing? Do you think this is a wise comment? How can this comment apply to your own life? Give a real-life example or make one up that fits this quote.

Prompt 10

Ed's eyes were drawn to the bright blue bottle on the table. Where had it come from? It wasn't there a minute ago.

Prompt 11

The top five most common street names in the United States are (in order) Second, Third, First, Fourth, and Park. (*First* isn't first on the list because the main streets are often called *Main*, *Center*, or named after someone.) Rename the top five streets. Choose any names you want. Explain why they would make good street names.

Prompt 12

David didn't see anyone, but he could hear them clearly. That's when David realized that something had happened to his hearing. He could hear through walls! He could hear people from a mile away!

Prompt 13

Compare yourself to a seal. Describe what is similar and different. Mention some advantages and disadvantages.

Prompt 14

"I need your help," said the little green man . . .

Prompt 15

You get to make three wishes come true, but they must be for someone else. Who would you give wishes to, what would you give them, and why?

Prompt 16

Nessie swung at the ball. Would it be another strike, or would she hit it?

Prompt 17

Your school can have either a new swimming pool or a new computer lab that all the students will get to use. What should they get and why? Give reasons for and against.

Prompt 18

Finally, it was the day Isaiah had been waiting for. The wait had been difficult, but at last it was over. Today . . .

Prompt 19

Describe four things that are north, east, south, and west of where you are right now. They can be objects, people, states, countries, or anything you want. Give at least two details about each of the four things.

Prompt 20

"All aboard!" yelled the conductor in his bright orange suit. "Put your face masks down. This is your last chance to get to the center of the Earth."

Prompt 21

You have been asked to entertain a five-year-old. Think of five things you can do with him or her that are age appropriate. One of the things should be reading aloud a particular book title.

Prompt 22

After hearing a loud noise, Lee dropped to his knees. "That was . . ."

Prompt 23

If you got a chance to go back in time to meet someone, who would you want to meet and why? What would you ask or say?

Prompt 24

There are two cookies on the table. One says, "BIG." The other says, "small." You reach out and carefully break off a piece of the . . .

Prompt 25

You get to open a store, restaurant, or service shop. What would you sell or serve? What would you name it? How would you decorate it? Where would you locate it, and what hours would it be open?

Prompt 26

"This worthless scribble is all your uncle left you," your mother said with anger. You look at the note, but then you realize it is a map with a code!

Prompt 27

You get to have a brand new pet—any kind or size you want. What would you get? What would you name it? What kinds of activities would you do with it?

Prompt 28

"Hey, watch where you step!" The voice is angry, but you can't tell who said it. Then you realize it is a small, speckled frog talking to you!

Prompt 29

New words are being added to the English language every year. For example, the word *cyberbullying* was recently added. Cyberbullying is the electronic posting of mean messages about a person. Make up a new word. Tell what it means. Then use it in a sentence. Your word can be silly, strange, or practical.

Prompt 30

You watched in fascination as the tornado twirled and swept toward you. Then, much to your amazement, you felt yourself being sucked in. You were no match for its power. The next thing you knew, you were being lifted far off the ground!

Prompt 31

You get to spend a day job shadowing. You can follow anyone you want for a whole day. Who would you follow and why? What do you hope to discover?

Prompt 32

It was Marie's last chance. The whole world was depending on her. Slowly and carefully, Marie . . .

Prompt 33

"If you put on those shoes, you won't be able to stop dancing," warned the strange-looking sales lady. "As if that's possible," thought Brian with amusement. Brian slipped on the shoes, laced them up, and then all of a sudden . . .

Prompt 34

As he peered over the side of the balloon basket, Rudy asked his friend Matt, "Should we land here?"

Prompt 35

Most spiders have four pairs of eyes. Imagine if you had eight eyes. Where would you place them? How would this change your life? Would you be better at some things than before?

Prompt 36

Tessa sat upright in bed and tried to hide the fear in her voice as she asked, "Is anybody there?"